MARILYN MONROE

IN THE MOVIES

MARILYN MONROE

IN THE MOVIES

A RETROSPECTIVE BY TIMOTHY KNIGHT

METRO BOOKS
NEW YORK

DESIGNER: Les Krantz with Julie Nor
CONTRIBUTING WRITERS:
Ken DuBois, Michael Fox, Pam Grady, Dennis Kwiatkowski, Sheila Lane,
Debra Ott, James Plath, Tim Sika and Christopher Varaste
COPY EDITOR: Katherine Hinkebein
PHOTO EDITOR: Chris Gore
EDITORIAL ASSISTANCE: Debbi Andrews
DVD DOCUMENTARY:
Les Krantz (Executive Producer), Jack Piantino (Video Editor)
Kristie Back (Musical Selections)

METRO BOOKS
122 Fifth Avenue
New York, NY 10011

ISBN-13: 978-1-4351-1857-7

Library of Congress data available on request

Printed and bound in China by PWGS

1 3 5 7 9 10 8 6 4 2

DEDICATION

For my parents,
William and Mary Ann Knight

ACKNOWLEDGMENTS

I received invaluable advice and assistance from many people while working on this book/documentary package. First and foremost, I am especially grateful to Les Krantz, my mentor and frequent collaborator, whose persistence and vision made *Marilyn Monroe in the Movies* possible. Thanks also to copy editor Katherine Hinkebein, designer Julie Nor and photo editor Chris Gore for their exemplary work. Kudos to Jack Piantino and Kristie Back for skillfully assembling and editing the accompanying documentary; to Jeff Joseph of Sabucat Productions for providing the feature film footage; to Susan Hormuth for providing the newsreel footage; and to Debbi Andrews for providing editorial assistance. Finally, my sincere thanks to everyone at Barnes & Noble for their good judgment and staunch support; I am especially indebted to Cynthia Barrett, Mark Levine and Peter Norton.

It was my great good fortune to work with a crackerjack team of writers on *Marilyn Monroe in the Movies*. I cannot thank them enough for their sterling contributions and prodigious work ethic. I tip my hat in gratitude to Ken Dubois, Michael Fox, Pam Grady, Dennis Kwiatkowski, Sheila Lane, Debra Ott, James Plath, Tim Sika and Christopher Varaste.

Scores of online and print sources were checked and cross-checked in the researching and writing of *Marilyn Monroe in the Movies*. Aside from the websites imdb.com, tcm.com and rottentomatoes.com, the New York Times online archive and the Academy Awards database, the following books provided the bulk of the information on Monroe's life and career: *Conversations With Wilder* by Cameron Crowe (Knopf, 1999); *The Many Lives of Marilyn Monroe* by Sarah Churchwell (Metropolitan Books, 2004); *Marilyn at Twentieth Century Fox* by Lawrence Crown (Comet Books. 1987); *The Marilyn Encyclopedia* by Adam Victor (The Overlook Press, 1999); *Marilyn Monroe* by Barbara Leaming (Three Rivers Press, 1998); and *Marilyn Monroe: The Biography* by Donald Spoto (HarperCollins, 1993).

TABLE OF CONTENTS

Introduction

W ith the arguable exception of Elvis Presley, no other star exerts a more enduring grip on the public's imagination than Marilyn Monroe. Like some luminescent butterfly she flitted across the screen, dazzling filmgoers worldwide, before dying young at age 36 — her image forever imprinted into our collective memory.

Why does this heartbreakingly beautiful and emotionally fragile star continue to haunt our dreams, nearly 50 years after her apparent suicide? It's a question that preoccupies academics, critics, film historians and legions of Monroe fans, who seemingly never tire of analyzing and documenting her life and career in exacting detail. Love goddess, dumb blonde, cultural icon, Dream Factory casualty — every year more labels get affixed to Monroe by writers alternately burnishing and deconstructing her legend as the greatest and most tragic of Hollywood sex symbols. Yet despite the scores of respectful biographies, lurid exposés, scholarly texts, gossipy articles and Internet websites devoted to Monroe, she nevertheless remains somewhat of an enigmatic figure

Monroe's Greatest Performances

Rose Loomis
Niagara (1953)

Monroe burns white hot as the sultry femme fatale in Henry Hathaway's *Niagara* (1953), an entertaining if overwrought melodrama co-starring Joseph Cotten and Jean Peters. A box office hit, *Niagara* was the first of three films released in 1953 that elevated Monroe to superstardom. A lesser actress would have played Rose as an outright villainess, but Monroe reveals glimmers of vulnerability beneath the character's wanton bravado.

Lorelei Lee
Gentlemen Prefer Blondes (1953)

Monroe is irresistibly charming as the likable gold digger in Howard Hawks' *Gentlemen Prefer Blondes* (1953), a buoyantly entertaining musical comedy. In the role Carol Channing originated on Broadway, Monroe sings and dances with breezy abandon, most famously Jule Styne and Leo Robin's "Diamonds Are a Girl's Best Friend." She also performs a winning duet with her co-star and fellow bombshell Jane Russell, "Two Little Girls from Little Rock."

The Girl
The Seven Year Itch (1955)

In *The Seven Year Itch* (1955), the first of two films she made with director Billy Wilder, Monroe is ideally cast as the curvy object of a middle-aged man's fantasies: beautiful, pliant and guileless. Her witty performance as the television commercial model innocently tempting a married sad sack led Wilder to proclaim her "an absolute genius as a comedic actress, with an extraordinary sense for comedic dialogue."

who defies ready categorization. Like all the truly great stars, Monroe retains her mystery, even as she reveals the sweetness and wounded vulnerability beneath her glamorous façade in films ranging from the hilarious comedy *Some Like It Hot* (1959) to the elegiac character study *The Misfits* (1961).

Although Monroe's chronic tardiness and paralyzing insecurities exasperated her directors and co-stars, none of them doubted her almost supernatural rapport with the camera — and the audience. John Huston, who directed Monroe in *The Asphalt Jungle* (1950) and *The Misfits*, said "She went right down into her own personal experience for everything, reached down and pulled something out of herself that was unique and extraordinary. She had no techniques. It was all the truth, it was only Marilyn. But it was Marilyn, plus. She found things, found things about womankind in herself."

Marilyn Monroe in the Movies pays tribute to this magical star, hailed by *Bus Stop* director Joshua Logan as "the most completely realized and authentic film actress since Garbo." Enjoy!

CHERIE
Bus Stop (1956)

Monroe silenced her critics with her touching and fully realized performance as a "hillbilly" saloon singer in Joshua Logan's film version of William Inge's 1955 Broadway play. Fresh from immersing herself in the Method acting techniques she learned at the Actors Studio, Monroe earned critical raves and a Golden Globe nomination for *Bus Stop* (1956), the first film she made for her Fox-based

SUGAR KANE KOWALCYZK
Some Like It Hot (1959)

Monroe sparkles as the unlucky-in-love singer/ukulele player who always gets the "fuzzy end of the lollipop" in her most beloved film, *Some Like It Hot* (1959). Sexy and beguiling, she manages the difficult feat of stealing scenes from Tony Curtis and Jack Lemmon, who give classic performances as cross-dressing musicians on the run from Chicago gangsters in Billy Wilder's masterpiece. Some

ROSLYN TABER
The Misfits (1961)

In her final completed film *The Misfits* (1961), Monroe gives a nuanced and sensitive performance as a Reno divorcee who gets involved with an over-the-hill cowboy (played by Monroe's childhood idol, Clark Gable). Playwright Arthur Miller wrote the role of Roslyn Taber expressly for Monroe, who spiraled downward into alcohol and prescription drug abuse during the film's production in Nevada

PART 1

1947-1952

MARILYN MONROE: 1947-1952

In 1947, Marilyn Monroe found herself with a six-month contract in hand from Twentieth Century Fox and the burning ambition to go along with it. As a contract player, she was sent to endless promotional events. Already an accomplished model, smiled her way through these assignments and befriended the press agents and reporters o would help her get noticed.

Eventually, her efforts led to being cast as a bit player in her first movie, *Scudda o! Scudda Hay!* (1948). This walk-on was followed by another bit part in *Dangerous rs* (1948). Unfortunately, neither of these films did much for Monroe's career and her ntract was dropped.

MONROE'S LEADING MEN, 1947-1952

GRANT
Business (1952)

st debonair star of Hollywood's era, Grant was equally at home n films, dramas, comedies and itchcock thrillers. Admired by his and directors, even the notori- anthrope Hitchcock, Grant was by *Monkey Business* director Hawks as "so far the best that n't anybody to be compared to *Monkey Business* was the fifth and m Grant made with Hawks who

STERLING HAYDEN
The Asphalt Jungle (1950)

No fan of Hollywood, Hayden reportedly claimed that he only made films to finance his true love: sailing the world's oceans. Initially promoted as "The Beautiful Blond Viking God" by Paramount Pictures, Hayden starred in a handful of classic films, including Nicholas Ray's *Johnny Guitar* (1954) and Stanley Kubrick's *The Killing* (1956). He later reteamed with Kubrick to portray the insane Brigadier General Jack D. Ripper

ROBERT RYAN
Clash by Night (1952)

Ryan made his name starring in gritty film noirs and westerns, but the stage-trained actor also did memorable work in *Lonelyhearts* (1958), an adaptation of Nathanael West's 1933 novel, and World War II films *The Longest Day* (1962) and *The Dirty Dozen* (1967). In 1973, the National Board of Review voted Ryan the Best Actor prize for his performance in *The Iceman Cometh* (1973) — one of four films Ryan made that year before dying

> "My first contract with Twentieth Century Fox was like my first vaccination. It didn't take."
>
> — Monroe

Low on funds, Monroe needed to land another studio contract. In March of 1948, she signed a six-month contract with Columbia Pictures. At Columbia she was given the second lead in *Ladies of the Chorus* (1949). To prepare her for the role, she was assigned to work with a vocal coach, Fred Karger, and an acting coach, Natasha Lytess. Monroe fell in love with the sophisticated Karger, but the relationship ended when he refused to marry her. Lytess, on the other hand, would go on to be Monroe's personal acting teacher for six more years.

Despite the help of these two professionals, Harry Cohn, the head of Columbia Pictures, was unimpressed with Monroe. He let her contract expire. Months of no work followed until Monroe landed a walk-on part in the last Marx Brothers' film, *Love Happy (1949)*. During these lean days, Monroe agreed to pose naked for a calendar shot by photographer Tom Kelley in May of 1949.

George Sanders
All About Eve (1950)

The screen's consummate snob, the English-born actor deservedly won an Academy Award for his snidely witty performance in *All About Eve* (1950). Although Sanders is most remembered for trading barbs with Bette Davis in Joseph L. Mankiewicz's classic film, he starred in dozens of films in a career spanning 43 years. In 1967, he made an especially vivid impression as the voice of the evil tiger Shere Khan in Walt Disney's *The Jungle Book*. Married four times – including separate trips to the altar with Zsa Zsa Gabor *and* her sister Magda — Sanders entitled his 1960 autobiography

David Wayne
We're Not Married (1952)

The Tony Award–winning actor made four films with Monroe in a two-year period: *As Young as You Feel* (1951), *Let's Get Married, O. Henry's Full House* (1952) and *How to Marry a Millionaire* (1953). Except for the 1951 remake of Fritz Lang's *M (1931)*, Wayne usually played supporting roles in film; he stole scenes from Spencer Tracy and Katharine Hepburn in *Adam's Rib* (1949) and held his own opposite Jack Lemmon and Walter Matthau in *The Front Page* (1974). Baby boomers of a certain age fondly recall Wayne's tongue-in-cheek performance as the Mad Hatter on the 1960 television

Richard Widmark
Don't Bother to Knock (1952)

After making a sensational, Academy Award-nominated debut as a psychopathic killer in *Kiss of Death* (1947), Widmark could have spent the rest of his career playing villains, but he wisely picked roles that showed his range: a public health officer fighting an epidemic in *Panic in the Streets* (1950); a Nazi war crimes prosecutor in *Judgment in Nuremberg* (1961); and a New York police detective in *Madigan* (1968). All told, Widmark starred in more than 60 films before retiring from acting in 1991.

In June of that year, she was off to New York to promote *Love Happy*. Although she was on-screen for less than two minutes, she made quite an impression with "the Marilyn Walk," an undulating gate that became her signature. The publicity she did for the film also brought her to the attention of *Life* magazine, which included her in a feature about starlets. She even parlayed the promotional buzz into a bit role in the Fox film *A Ticket to Tomahawk (1950)*. Most importantly, *Love Happy* brought her to the attention of Johnny Hyde.

Johnny Hyde was a top agent at the William Morris Agency when he met Monroe in Palm Springs. He was 53 years old and married at the time, but he fell madly in love with Monroe. He is credited for igniting Monroe's career by getting her an audition with John Huston for his film, *The Asphalt Jungle* (1950). The film gave Monroe her largest part yet and received strong reviews.

That same year, three other movies were released in which Monroe played a role, *Right Cross, The Fireball* and *All About Eve*. The first two came and went without much fanfare, but *All About Eve,* directed by Joseph L. Mankiewicz, became a classic. Although Monroe had a small role, she held her own with Academy Award winners Bette Davis and Anne Baxter. Darryl Zanuck took notice and offered Monroe a new

"She wanted to be an actress and a movie star. I knew nothing could stop her. The drive and determination and need inside Marilyn could not be halted."

— Sidney Skolsky, Hollywood syndicated columnist, feature writer and reporter

Opposite page: Monroe as the aspiring actress Miss Caswell in *All About Eve* (1950). Top: Anne Bancroft, Monroe and Richard Widmark in *Don't Bother to Knock* (1952).

six-month contract at Twentieth Century Fox. Johnny Hyde negotiated the deal and died one week later. Monroe was devastated.

Back at Fox, Monroe pulled herself together to make several comedies, *As Young as You Feel* (1951), *Love Nest* (1951) and *Let's Make It Legal* (1951). An industrial film she made for MGM about General Motors was also released that year, *Hometown Story*. Six months went by and Monroe's contract was up. She turned to a new agent, Hugh French, for help. He secured a new, seven-year deal. However, many believe it was not French that sealed the deal, but a show-stopping appearance Marilyn made at a Fox party for its exhibitors.

Around this time, Fox loaned out Monroe to RKO to make *Clash by Night* (1952). The film gave Marilyn a dramatic role; however, the real theatrics began when a reporter, Aline Mosby, learned about Monroe's nude calendar shoot in 1949. The Fox executives panicked. Monroe was told to deny the whole thing, but she refused. When asked by Mosby why she did it, Monroe replied, "I was broke and needed the money." It could have been a disaster, but instead it was a publicity coup that spurred ticket sales for *Clash by Night* and elevated Monroe's profile. Nineteen fifty-two also saw the release of three other Monroe films, *O. Henry's Full House, Monkey Business* and *Don't Bother to Knock,* but the film that would bring her to the next level was yet to come.

LADIES OF THE CHORUS (1949)

COLUMBIA PICTURES

DIRECTOR: PHIL KARLSON

SCREENPLAY: JOSEPH CAROLE AND HARRY SAUBER

STORY: SAUBER

PRINCIPAL CAST: ADELE JERGENS (MAY MARTIN), MARILYN MONROE (PEGGY MARTIN), RAND BROOKS (RANDY CARROLL), NANA BRYANT (MRS. CARROLL), EDDIE GARR (BILLY MACKAY), BILL REYNOLDS (ALAN WAKEFIELD), AND MARJORIE HOSHELLE (BUBBLES LaRUE)

The antithetical worlds of burlesque and high society converge in *Ladies of the Chorus* (1949), which features Marilyn Monroe in the sole leading role she played during her six-month Columbia Pictures contract. The 23-year-old starlet would also receive above-the-title billing for the first time in her career — albeit just in the advertising campaign for *Ladies of the Chorus*, directed with crisp efficiency by B-movie filmmaker Phil Karlson.

In this cliché-ridden but engaging programmer, Monroe plays Peggy Martin, a chorus girl hoofing it alongside her overprotective mother Mae (Adele Jergens), a former burlesque queen. When headliner Bubbles LaRue (Marjorie Hoshelle), a.k.a "Queen of the Quivers," refuses to go on one night, Peggy takes her place — and becomes an instant burlesque sensation.

As Peggy's star ascends on the burlesque circuit, she attracts the attention of wealthy playboy Randy Carroll (Rand Brooks), who begins sending orchids to her

Top: Monroe (far left) as Peggy Martin, chorus girl turned burlesque queen. Bottom: A star is born: Peggy performs "Anyone Can Tell I Love You."

dressing room nightly. A whirlwind romance ensues between the playboy and the burlesque star, much to the alarm of Peggy's mother, Mae. For as she reveals to Peggy, Mae long ago married into high society herself, only to be shunned once her past was exposed: "Everybody treated me like a queen — until they found out I was a queen. A *burlesque* queen."

After her wealthy husband's family had the marriage annulled, and Peggy was born four months later, Mae returned to burlesque — not as the star but as one of the ladies of the chorus. However, she agrees to give her blessing to Peggy's marriage if Randy first tells his mother about her prospective daughter-in-law's line of work. In true B-movie fashion, word of Peggy's showbiz career leaks out during the engagement party, but to the surprise of everyone, Randy's mother (Nana Bryant) makes her own surprise announcement, paving the way for the film's conclusion.

Before filming of *Ladies of the Chorus* got underway in March of 1948, Monroe underwent electrolysis to have her hairline raised. She also had her ash blonde hair lightened to platinum, and had cosmetic dentistry to correct her protruding front teeth. The transformation from pretty Norma Jeane Baker to screen siren Marilyn Monroe had begun in earnest.

Shot in 10 days flat, *Ladies of the Chorus* gave moviegoers their first hint of Monroe's musical talents, which she displays with charming aplomb in the film's

Top: Peggy meets her secret admirer Randy Carroll (Rand Brooks). Bottom: Peggy's mother, Mae (Adele Jergens), struts her stuff. A former Rockette, Jergens worked steadily in B-movies throughout the 1940s and 1950s.

burlesque sequences. According to Susan Doll's 2007 article "Marilyn Monroe's Early Career" for the website HowStuffWorks.com, the film's musical director Fred Karger worked patiently with Monroe to ease her jitters and improve her singing voice (they also briefly dated). Thanks to Karger, Monroe performs two musical numbers, "Anyone Can Tell I Love You" and "Every Baby Needs a Da-Da Daddy" with an ease and confidence that belies her inexperience.

Monroe also does fine work in the dramatic scenes opposite Jergens, a former Rockette improbably playing Monroe's mother; Jergens was just nine years older than Monroe. The two women reportedly shared at least one thing in common: comedian Milton Berle, who claimed in his 1974 autobiography that he had an affair with Monroe while romantically linked with Jergens.

Whereas Monroe's reported liaison with Berle was no more than a fling, her relationship with Columbia's head drama coach Natasha Lytess lasted six years. Monroe met Lytess, a character actress and former student of renowned Austrian stage and film director Max Reinhardt, during the filming of *Ladies of the Chorus*.

"Peggy doesn't belong in your world. She belongs in the show world — burlesque. 'Burlesque Queen'— that's what people call her."

— Mae Martin (Adele Jergens)

By all accounts a demanding taskmaster, Lytess exerted considerable influence over her malleable protégé; as Lytess once quipped, "Marilyn needed me like a dead man needs a coffin." The two would work closely together, often to the frustration of Monroe's directors, until *The Seven Year Itch* (1955).

Monroe also formed an enduring and far less controversial bond with costume designer Jean-Louis while making *Ladies of the Chorus*. The French-born head designer for the studio, Jean-Louis would later design Monroe's wardrobe for *The Misfits* (1961) and the uncompleted *Something's Got to Give* (1962), as well as the infamous skin-tight, silk gown she wore to sing "Happy Birthday" to President John F. Kennedy at his 45th birthday celebration in 1962.

Although Monroe won praise for her "nifty warbling" and "nice personality" from *Variety*'s critic, Columbia Pictures studio chief Harry Cohn was reportedly unimpressed with her performance in *Ladies of the Chorus* and didn't renew her six-month contract. Widely reviled as the most tyrannical and cutthroat of the era's studio moguls, Cohn apparently decreed that Monroe lacked the elusive "It" factor to become a major star, like the studio's top sex symbol, Rita Hayworth. Of course, Monroe's refusal to spend the weekend with Cohn on his yacht may have prompted him to drop her from the studio roster out of spite, rather than her alleged lack of star quality. Whatever the reason, Cohn would soon regret his rash decision to release Monroe from her Columbia contract.

Clocking in at a compact 61 minutes, *Ladies of the Chorus* is an enjoyable diversion, a solid and serviceable cross between radio soap opera and musical comedy. The entire cast is uniformly fine, with notable turns by Jergens, Brooks, Bryant and veteran nightclub entertainer and radio personality Eddie Garr (father of comic actress Teri Garr) as Billy Mackay, Mae Martin's burlesque partner. But it is Monroe who ultimately shines brightest in *Ladies of the Chorus,* in a winning performance that offers tantalizing hints of her magical screen persona.

"I kept driving past the theater with my name on the marquee. Was I excited. I wished they were using 'Norma Jeane' so that all the kids at the home and schools who never noticed me could see it."

— Monroe, on seeing her name above the title for *Ladies of the Chorus*

"One of the bright spots is Miss Monroe's singing. She is pretty, and with her pleasing voice and style, she shows promise."

— *Motion Picture Herald*

THE ASPHALT JUNGLE (1950)

MGM

DIRECTOR: JOHN HUSTON

SCREENPLAY: JOHN HUSTON AND BEN MADDOW

BASED ON THE NOVEL BY W. R. BURNETT

PRINCIPAL CAST: STERLING HAYDEN (DIX HANDLEY), LOUIS CALHERN (ALONZO EMMERICH), DOROTHY TREE (MAY EMMERICH), JEAN HAGEN (DOLL CONOVAN), JAMES WHITMORE (GUS MINISSI), SAM JAFFE (DOC ERWIN RIEDENSCHNEIDER), BARRY KELLEY (LIEUTENANT DITRICH), ANTHONY CARUSO (LOUIS CIAVELLI), MARC LAWRENCE (COBBY) AND MARILYN MONROE (ANGELA PHINLAY)

In the first three years of her fledgling film career, Marilyn Monroe appeared in half a dozen minor roles, sometimes without receiving billing. But inside the industry she was building a name for herself, and the determined starlet's perseverance paid off when John Huston cast Monroe in his film noir crime thriller, *The Asphalt Jungle*. Having won Academy Awards for Best Director and Best Screenplay for *The Treasure of Sierra Madre* (1948), Huston was then at the peak of his popularity. For any young actor in 1950, the opportunity to work with Huston was a celluloid dream come true.

Based on Huston's landmark films with Humphrey Bogart — in addition to *The Treasure of Sierra Madre*, they had also made *The Maltese Falcon* (1941) and *Key Largo* (1948) — 1950-era audiences had come to expect stark realism from Huston, and *The Asphalt Jungle* did not disappoint them. Filmed in a treeless Los Angeles warehouse district, the narrative unfolds against a bleak

Top: Gus (James Whitmore) agrees to help Dix (Sterling Hayden) with his gambling debts. Bottom: Emmerich (Louis Calhern) tells Cobby (Marc Lawrence) about his plan to fence the stolen jewels.

backdrop, a landscape deserted except for slowly rolling patrol cars and criminals slinking through the shadows. The underground world is home to a variety of types, each motivated by some form of vice, but they're quickly united when the famous criminal Doc Erwin Riedenschneider (Sam Jaffe) is released from prison and hits the street looking to assemble a crew. Doc is planning a can't-miss jewelry heist — his last big score — and he starts by securing pre-heist financing from Alonzo Emmerich (Louis Calhern), a crooked attorney who's stretching himself thin by lavishing luxury on both his wife (Dorothy Tree) and his young girlfriend, Angela (Marilyn Monroe). As his right-hand man, Doc brings on Dix Handley (Sterling Hayden), a tough hooligan with his own moral code and a weakness for horses. Gus Minissi (James Whitmore), a diner owner who's only slightly legit, becomes the driver for the heist, along with family man and safecracker Louis Ciavelli (Anthony Caruso). The plan is perfect, Doc assures them, and the take is a million dollars in jewels. But every one of them has a different idea about how much of that money will be theirs.

The premise of a seasoned criminal trying to make one last heist is undeniably appealing; it became the foundation for countless caper films in the decades to come, including three more versions of *The Asphalt Jungle*, one of them a western. But the gorgeous cinematography, crisp dialogue, and impeccable casting make *The Asphalt Jungle* one of a kind. Sterling Hayden, playing the sensitive loner Dix, is fascinating to watch as

Top: Monroe as Angela Phinlay, Emmerich's gorgeous young mistress. Bottom: Monroe kept acting coach Natasha Lytess close on the set of *The Asphalt Jungle*.

he twists his stubbled face and gazes off, dreaming of better days. As Doc, a master of self-control, Sam Jaffe generates intensity while barely raising his voice above a whisper. James Whitmore, who later achieved his greatest renown for playing Harry S. Truman and Will Rogers in one-man shows, cuts a surprisingly menacing figure as Gus. Other supporting cast members are memorable as well, including Jean Hagen as Dix's friend Doll, a broken-down wreck with a heartbreaking smile; Marc Lawrence as the bookie Cobby, a tough talker who crumbles when the pressure's on; and Barry Kelley as Lieutenant Ditrich, who leans on the local criminals just enough to make a buck.

The Asphalt Jungle would turn out to be Monroe's big break, yet it almost never happened. She initially gave a poor audition for Huston, who was already disinclined to cast her because he'd decided on Lola Albright for the part of Angela Phinlay. But MGM talent director Lucille Ryman Carroll told Huston that Albright would cost $1,500 a week, almost five times the amount budgeted for the small role, and suggested Monroe might be a good fit, and at a fraction of the cost. Still, he tested eight other actresses for the role, but Carroll continued to push for Monroe and

Dix reminisces about better days growing up on his family's Kentucky farm.

"Haven't you bothered me enough, you big banana-head?"

—— Angela Phinlay (Monroe) to police officer

eventually convinced Huston, who admitted that she was adequate but more impressive off screen than when the cameras rolled.

On the set, Monroe relied heavily on her personal acting coach, Natasha Lytess, but in the finished film, she betrays no trace of nervousness or insecurity. In fact, the confident sexuality she exudes is startling and new, and in its way as revolutionary as the gritty, unvarnished realism Huston was bringing to the film overall. The viewer's first glimpse of Monroe as Angela is essentially from her lover's point of view, looking down at her, curled up on a couch. She opens her eyes and sleepily asks, "What's the big idea, standing there staring at me...?" There's a salacious and sad undercurrent to the scene, due to the actors' age difference — Monroe was 24 and Calhern 55 — which Huston reemphasizes in a later scene, when Angela bubbles excitedly about vacation plans while her exhausted older lover looks on. In another remarkable scene, Angela finds herself caught up in the crime and frantically weighs her options; it's a wonderful showcase for Monroe's dramatic talents, which were already developed and too often overlooked.

When it opened in the spring of 1950, *The Asphalt Jungle* was a sensation. Audiences found it exciting, artful, and new, and the film industry recognized it as a breakthrough for realistic filmmaking. It received Academy Award nominations for Best Director for Huston, Best Screenplay for Huston and Ben Maddow, Best Black-and-White Cinematography for Harold Rosson, and Best Supporting Actor for Sam Jaffe. For his directorial achievement, Huston was also nominated for a Golden Globe and a Directors Guild of America award. Despite the

Top: Doc (Sam Jaffe) explains his plan for the million-dollar jewel heist. Bottom: The heist is underway: Doc and Dix watch Louis Ciavelli (Anthony Caruso) crack the safe.

fact that her billing was buried in the movie's end credits, audiences took note of Monroe as well, including *Photoplay* reviewer Liza Wilson who singled her out by noting, "There's a beautiful blonde, name of Marilyn Monroe. She makes the most of her footage."

With *The Asphalt Jungle,* Monroe's career shifted into high gear; by the end of the year she had made three more films and acted alongside Bette Davis in *All About Eve.* The public's fascination with Monroe had begun, and film executives were starting to see her box office potential. The "beautiful blonde" was on her way to Hollywood superstardom.

"One way or another, we all work for our vice."

— Doc Riedenschneider (Sam Jaffe) to Cobby (Marc Lawrence)

"Experience has taught me never to trust a policeman. Just when you think one's all right, he turns legit."

— Doc Riedenschneider (Sam Jaffe) to Cobby (Marc Lawrence)

Crime is only a left-handed form of human endeavor."

— Alonzo Emmerich (Louis Calhern) to May Emmerich (Dorothy Tree)

Opposite page: Angela's excited to learn that Emmerich is sending her away on a luxury vacation. Top: Caught up in the plot, Angela angrily confronts a police officer at her bedroom door. Bottom: Dix's mug shot. Twenty-two years later, Hayden portrayed the corrupt police captain in *The Godfather* (1972).

All About Eve (1950)

Twentieth Century Fox

Director: Joseph L. Mankiewicz

Screenplay: Joseph L. Mankiewicz

Based on the short story "The Wisdom of Eve" by Mary Orr

Principal Cast: Bette Davis (Margo Channing), Anne Baxter (Eve Harrington), George Sanders (Addison DeWitt), Celeste Holm (Karen Richards), Gary Merrill (Bill Sampson), Hugh Marlowe (Lloyd Richards), Thelma Ritter (Birdie), Gregory Ratoff (Max Fabian) and Marilyn Monroe (Miss Caswell)

Nineteen fifty was a breakthrough year for 24-year-old starlet Marilyn Monroe, who impressed audiences and critics alike with eye-catching performances in two radically different films: John Huston's gritty crime drama *The Asphalt Jungle* and Joseph L. Mankiewicz's acerbically witty valentine to Broadway, *All About Eve*. Based on Mary Orr's short story "The Wisdom of Eve," *All About Eve* features Monroe in yet another small but vivid role opposite Hollywood grande dame Bette Davis, then making a comeback after the debacle of the camp melodrama *Beyond the Forest* (1949). They join an impressive cast of seasoned actors, including Anne Baxter, George Sanders, Celeste Holm, Gary Merrill and Thelma Ritter, in 1950's Academy Award winner for Best Picture, ranked number 16 in the American Film Institute's 1998 poll of the 100 greatest American films.

Top: "Fasten your seat belts, it's going to be a bumpy night."Broadway star Margo Channing (Bette Davis) "fed up" with her scheming assistant, Eve Harrington (Anne Baxter).Bottom: In heady company: Monroe with Academy Award winners Anne Baxter, Bette Davis and George Sanders in *All About Eve*'s classic party scene.

Reportedly inspired by a true story involving Austrian actress Elisabeth Bergner, *All About Eve* revolves around the machinations of Eve Harrington (Anne Baxter), the ambitious assistant to Broadway star Margo Channing (Bette Davis). A cunning, ruthless schemer, Eve infiltrates Margo's inner circle, making herself indispensable to the actress while clawing and backstabbing her way into the spotlight. Leaving a trail of betrayals and frayed relationships in her wake, Eve may realize her dream of headlining a Broadway play by acclaimed playwright Lloyd Richards (Hugh Marlowe), but she soon meets her match in vitriolic theatre critic Addison DeWitt (George Sanders, in an Oscar-winning performance).

A Hollywood triple threat, writer-director-producer Joseph L. Mankiewicz deservedly won an Academy Award for his *All About Eve* screenplay, which gives Davis one of her greatest roles as the sharp-tongued yet likable diva Margo Channing, tossing off quips between martinis. Although she would go on to make such hits as *Whatever Happened to Baby Jane?* (1962) and *Hush…Hush, Sweet Charlotte* (1964), *All About Eve* represents a career high for her co-stars Baxter, Holm, Sanders, Marlowe and Merrill (Davis' real-life husband). During filming, however, neither Davis nor her co-stars could foresee that the ninth-billed Monroe was destined to become a cinematic icon.

Cast as the comely and dim Miss Claudia Caswell, Monroe plays the obvious foil to the duplicitous Eve.

Top: Miss Caswell (Monroe) charms Broadway producer Max Fabian (Gregory Ratoff). Bottom: Miss Caswell with her vitriolic escort, theatre critic Addison DeWitt (Sanders).

Ironically, Monroe's career would follow a similar trajectory to the title character's after the film's release. Like Eve, the starlet's presence on set also raised the ire of the female cast while earning the director's praise and sympathy. Monroe was Mankiewicz's first choice and he would later state that "there was a breathlessness and sort of glued-on innocence that I found appealing." He was met with opposition from studio chief Darryl Zanuck, who had fired Marilyn from her contract at Twentieth Century Fox. After much coaxing from Monroe's lover Johnny Hyde, the top agent at William Morris, Zanuck relented and Monroe was hired for $500 a week. Joining ranks with a cinematic giant like Davis gave Monroe a much-needed career boost and she would remain at Twentieth Century Fox for the duration of her career.

Unfortunately, the issues that would plague the actress throughout her life began to surface on the first day of shooting in Los Angeles, where she kept cast and crew waiting for over an hour on a soundstage. Her whispered apologies prompted Russian character actor Gregory Ratoff to gush, "That girl is going to be a big star!" A miffed Celeste Holm reportedly snapped, "Why? Because she kept us all waiting an hour?"

Holm also took issue with the bright satin gown Charles LeMaire had designed for Monroe, since the rest of the women were clad in muted cocktail-hour dresses. With crew in place, Mankiewicz motioned the cameras and Monroe stepped forward with a surprising air of authority. She then proceeded to upstage Davis and Baxter in the claustrophobic confines of the staircase set. Introduced as "a graduate of the Copacabana School of Dramatic Art"

Make way for a diva: Miss Caswell wisely gives Margo Channing a wide berth. Opposite page: Monroe beat out ten actresses for the small but eye-catching role of Miss Caswell in *All About Eve*.

by chaperone Addison DeWitt, Miss Caswell may be eye candy, but Monroe plays her with a surprising degree of self-possession. Her effortless sensuality — what Billy Wilder later called Monroe's "flesh impact" — commands the screen, even in the midst of scene stealer par excellence, Bette Davis.

Monroe's nuanced and wide-eyed delivery also reveals an innate flair for comic timing, an artistry that was overlooked by her co-stars. Deriding the actress's overt sexuality in her 1976 memoir *Intermission*, Anne Baxter recalled working with Monroe on an earlier project, *A Ticket to Tomahawk* (1950), just prior to *All About Eve*: "Marilyn Monroe came in with a different crew member every night, wearing the same sweater. She was eminently braless and I particularly remember the pink V-necked angora sweater. It was said she slept in it." Interviewed in 1978, Celeste Holm remained equally dismissive in her recollections: "I confess I saw nothing special about her Betty Boop quality. I thought she was quite sweet and terribly dumb, and my natural reaction was, 'Whose girl is that?'"

Marilyn Monroe's final scene in *All About Eve* takes place in the lobby of a fictitious New York theatre where she's stopped auditioning due to a nervous stomach, or as Addison puts it, "being violently ill to her tummy." Woozily slinking out of the ladies room, Monroe maximizes her few seconds of screen time by languidly moving as if in slow motion. This bit of showmanship prompted Davis to sneer, "She thinks if she can wiggle her ass and coo away, she can carry a scene."

If Monroe's appeal was lost on Davis, Mankiewicz recognized the starlet as much more than the sum of her curves. In his book *More About All About Eve*, the director offers a poignant reminiscence of the neophyte screen goddess: "I thought of her, then, as the loneliest person I had ever known. Throughout our location period in San Francisco, Marilyn would be spotted at one restaurant or another dining alone. Or drinking alone. We'd always ask her to join us, and she would, and seemed pleased, but somehow she never understood or accepted our assumption that she was one of us. She remained alone. She was not a loner. She was just *alone*."

"Why do they always look like unhappy rabbits?"

- Miss Caswell (Monroe) on Broadway producers

LOVE NEST (1951)

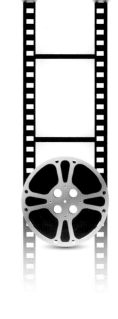

TWENTIETH CENTURY FOX

DIRECTOR: JOSEPH M. NEWMAN

SCREENPLAY: I.A.L. DIAMOND

BASED ON THE NOVEL "THE RELUCTANT LANDLORD" BY SCOTT CORBETT

PRINCIPAL CAST: WILLIAM LUNDIGAN (JIM SCOTT), MARILYN MONROE (ROBERTA "BOBBY" STEVENS), JUNE HAVER (CONNIE SCOTT), FRANK FAY (CHARLIE PATTERSON), JACK PAAR (ED FORBES) AND LEATRICE JOY (EADIE GAYNOR)

An underrated comic gem, *Love Nest* earned Marilyn Monroe some of her first positive notices for her brief but vivid turn in the second film she made under her renegotiated Fox contract. Written by I.A.L. Diamond, who later collaborated with director Billy Wilder on such classics as *Some Like It Hot* (1959) and *The Apartment* (1960), this unpretentious charmer showcases Monroe's burgeoning star quality to full advantage.

Directed by Joseph M. Newman, whose lengthy Hollywood career dated back to the silent era, *Love Nest* is based on Scott Corbett's 1950 novel, *The Reluctant Landlord*. Fox contract player William Lundigan stars as Jim Scott, a serviceman returning to his New York hometown from Paris, where he nurtured his literary ambitions. Eager to reunite with his wife, Connie (June Haver), and begin writing the great American novel, Jim is surprised to learn that she's used up all their savings to

Top: New tenant Roberta "Bobby" Stevens (Monroe) arrives to stir things up in *Love Nest*. Bottom: Ed Forbes (Jack Paar) wastes no time in putting the moves on Bobby.

buy a run-down apartment building. In Connie's grand plan for their future, she and Jim will live in a converted basement apartment and rent out the other apartments she's furnished with inherited antiques.

Although he tries to share Connie's enthusiasm for her moneymaking venture, Jim is less than thrilled by the prospect of playing landlord to his eccentric tenants and constantly making repairs to the money pit of a building. Nor does he have much time to devote to writing, except for the quickie magazine articles he churns out to pay the bills. In a last-ditch desperate effort to stay solvent, Jim invites his old army buddy Bobby to rent an apartment. But when Bobby turns out to be Roberta Stevens (Monroe), Connie is immediately suspicious of Jim's friendship with the shapely WAC. To make matters worse, FBI agents show up one day, asking questions about one of the tenants, Charley Patterson (Frank Fay). Fortunately for Jim and Connie, all the many loose ends get tied up neatly in time for the film's upbeat conclusion.

While not one of the studio's "A-list" productions, *Love Nest* boasts a roster of top-caliber talent behind the camera. In addition to Diamond who later won the Academy Award for Best Original Screenplay for co-writing *The Apartment* (1960) with Wilder, the film features the work of two veteran craftsmen: cinematographer Lloyd Ahern (*Miracle on 34th Street*) and legendary art director Lyle R. Wheeler (*Gone with the Wind*), who racked up a staggering 29

Top: "I'd like to inspect the premises." Ed tries again with Bobby. Bottom: Caption: Bobby discovers a guest asleep on her couch.

Academy Award nominations during his career (he won the golden statuette five times). Thanks to Ahern and Wheeler, *Love Nest* has the look and feel of a major Fox release, rather than a minor film starring studio contract players.

As for the cast, Lundigan and Haver make an appealing team in *Love Nest*, one of the last films Haver made before she announced her plans to retire from acting and become a nun (she later married Fred MacMurray and steered clear of the convent). Vaudeville and radio performer Frank Fay and silent screen actress Leatrice Joy also contribute winning performances as two of the more

The famous shower sequence with Monroe lasts only seconds on-screen but stirred up lots of interest on the set during filming. Opposite page: Connie Scott (June Haver) gently breaks the news of her latest purchase to husband Jim (William Lundigan).

colorful tenants in the building. Another member of the film's supporting cast, Jack Paar, would achieve greater success six years later, as the host of *The Tonight Show* from 1957 to 1962. No fan of Monroe — he once likened her to a "frightened waitress in a diner," according to Susan Doll's 2007 article "Monroe's Early Career" for HowStuffWorks.com — Paar nastily dismissed his co-star as an intellectual poseur, carrying Marcel Proust novels he believed she never read. But as Doll reports, Monroe *was* taking literature and art history courses at UCLA during the filming of *Love Nest*, so Paar's remarks about her were probably just spiteful conjecture.

Although Monroe doesn't have a lot of screen time in *Love Nest*, she's funny

"It seems strange giving money to a man you know."

— Roberta Stevens (Monroe) to her landlord in *Love Nest*

33

Top: The sexpot alone — for
now. Bottom: The landlords
with their busybody tenant,
Mrs. Arnold (Maude Wallace).

and sexy as Roberta. In his shared DVD commentary track with *Love Nest* director Newman, film historian Jack Allen notes that Monroe easily passes the litmus test of stardom, even at this early stage in her career: You cannot take your eyes off her whenever she appears.

Monroe works her magic in *Love Nest*.

She projects that irresistible mixture of smoldering sexuality and childlike sweetness that set her apart from all screen sirens. In fact, Monroe's allure was so potent on and off screen that Newman shot her character's shower scene on a closed set. According to Hollywood columnist Sidney Skolsky, "You could hear the

electricity" when Monroe undressed to film the eye-catching scene.

That "electricity" would jump-start Monroe's rise to stardom. A year after making *Love Nest*, she would be working with superstars Barbara Stanywck and Cary Grant in *Clash by Night* (1952) and *Monkey Business* (1952), respectively.

"Love Youth? Love Excitement? Love Rollicking Fun? Then You'll Most Certainly Love *Love Nest*!

— from the trailer

Opposite page: Mrs. Arnold, makes a startling observation that could lead to very serious repercussions for her landlords Connie and Jim. Top: Connie attempts to assure Jim that everything will be fine. Bottom: June Haver as Connie Scott. A devout Roman Catholic, Haver reportedly considered becoming a nun, but later married actor Fred MacMurray and retired from acting.

LET'S MAKE IT LEGAL (1951)

TWENTIETH CENTURY FOX

DIRECTOR: RICHARD SALE

SCREENPLAY: I.A.L. DIAMOND AND F. HUGH HERBERT

BASED ON A STORY BY MORTIMER BRAUS

PRINCIPAL CAST: CLAUDETTE COLBERT (MIRIAM HALSWORTH), MACDONALD CAREY (HUGH HALSWORTH), ZACHARY SCOTT (VICTOR MACFARLAND), ROBERT WAGNER (JERRY DENHAM), BARBARA BATES (BARBARA DENHAM) AND MARILYN MONROE (JOYCE MANNERING)

Strictly an in-house production for Twentieth Century Fox, conceived, written and directed by studio contractees, *Let's Make It Legal* was never meant to be more than an innocuous piece of fluff. Yet nearly 60 years after its release, Richard Sale's romantic comedy holds up surprisingly well, due to a lucky combination of winning elements: a witty screenplay co-written by I.A.L. Diamond, who later formed an Academy Award–winning partnership with director Billy Wilder; assured direction by Sale; and superb casting that paired established stars with talented studio players-in-training — most notably Marilyn Monroe, who would soon become the biggest movie star in the world.

Based on a story by Mortimer Braus, Diamond and co-writer F. Hugh Herbert's screenplay milks a dysfunctional family scenario for laughs. Weary of her husband's incessant gambling Miriam Halsworth (Claudette Colbert) throws him out; now she's happily

Top: Hugh Halsworth (Macdonald Carey) explains to his son-in-law Jerry Denham (Robert Wagner) that his wife was the one who called it quits. Bottom: Fortune-seeker Joyce Mannering (Monroe) asks Hugh Halsworth to introduce her to his millionaire acquaintance.

counting down the last few days before the divorce is official. But her jilted husband Hugh (Macdonald Carey) doesn't seem to know that's he's been ejected, so he's back at the house every day, tending to his prized rose bushes, lounging on the patio, or changing clothes in the front hallway.

Sharing the house are the couple's grown daughter Barbara (Barbara Bates), her baby, and her husband Jerry (Robert Wagner), who is ready to move out of his in-laws' place the moment his wife gives the nod. Jerry works for Hugh in the luxury hotel's public relations department, but his loyalty stops at the office; at home, Jerry hopes to get his mother-in-law remarried as soon as possible so he and his family can start their own life somewhere else.

Jerry sees his opportunity when wealthy gadfly Victor Macfarland (Zachary Scott) returns to town. An old flame of Miriam's, Victor has never gotten over the fact that she turned him down to marry Hugh. When Victor finds out she's about to become available again, he moves in quickly, showering her with elaborate gifts and courting her brazenly, even while Hugh lingers at the edge of the scene. As the perpetually unwanted guest, forever traipsing through the house with his pruning shears, Hugh has little to say in the matter, and the best idea he can conjure is to push a young model in Victor's direction. But even the beautiful Joyce Mannering (Marilyn Monroe) can't distract Victor from his ultimate conquest: winning back the girl who got away.

Top: The celebrated Victor Macfarland (Zachary Scott) basks in reporters' attention. Bottom: Miriam Halsworth (Claudette Colbert) is shocked to discover that her soon-to-be ex-husband Hugh keeps a change of clothes in her front hall closet.

A veteran of almost 60 films by the time she made *Let's Make It Legal*, Claudette Colbert knows exactly how to bring out the humor in the script and in her co-stars as well; she gives them room to work. Her leading man Macdonald Carey, best known today for starring in the long-running NBC soap opera *Days of Our Lives*, reveals himself to be a fine comic actor, as does Zachary Scott, a versatile actor who excelled at playing heavies and romantic leads. In one of his few comedies, Scott is hilarious as the narcissistic Victor, who alternates between fawning over Miriam and throwing temper tantrums when he doesn't get his way.

Whereas Colbert, Carey and Scott had spent years in front of the camera, their co-stars were still figuring out how to maximize their assets on-screen. Bates had created a stir with her small but pivotal role in the closing scenes of *All About Eve* (1950). As for Wagner, he's surprisingly polished in only his third feature film.

Although she has comparatively far less screen time than Bates and Wagner, Monroe brings a light comic touch to her scenes in the beginning, middle and end of *Let's Make It Legal*. The role was created for her in part because of public demand,

Three's company: Hugh's unfazed by Victor's attempts to woo Miriam.

"You don't believe in the sanctity of divorce, do you?"

— Miriam Halsworth (Claudette Colbert) to Hugh Halsworth (Macdonald Carey)

as the studio's press department was deluged with fan letters for Monroe; her photograph had become a popular pin-up with U.S. servicemen in Korea. Despite her obvious acting skills, Monroe's *Let's Make It Legal* character was contrived to put her physical beauty on display; she appears in a swimsuit and other revealing outfits, and poses silently for most of her time on-screen. At one point, a character crudely refers to her as a small-town beauty pageant winner trying to get ahead by "posing for cheesecake."

The entire cast of *Let's Make It Legal* was under contract to Twentieth Century Fox, and all were bound by a straightforward agreement: they would appear in the roles and films chosen for them or take a "suspension" from work while the film was made. For *Let's Make It Legal* the work schedule was 9 a.m. to 6 p.m. Monday through Friday. Filming took place almost exclusively on the studio lot, and the cast's duties included a publicity tour in which the actors appeared on stage, singing songs and telling jokes to movie theater crowds. But the system had advantages. The actors, including established stars whose box office clout was waning, had steady work, and newcomers had a chance to learn virtually every part of how a film is made. They had Darryl Zanuck as well, who ran the studio, but who also kept a hand in many creative decisions and hand-picked many of the young actors who came to the studio to be trained and groomed.

Reminiscing about the filming of *Let's Make It Legal* more than half a century later, Robert Wagner called it one of the happiest times of his life, in large part because of the camaraderie and affection he felt from the cast and crew. Wagner was 21 years old when he made the film

Top: Joyce Mannering implores Hugh to introduce her to Victor. Bottom: Joyce turns on the charm for Victor.

— Monroe a few years older — and both were among the stable of young actors under studio contract, working hard, learning the trade and hoping for leading roles. As they worked their way through the system, Wagner and Monroe did screen tests together and traveled on publicity tours, and he remembered her as kind, caring and emotional, and unprepared for the celebrity that followed. "We were all knocking around, trying to get started in the picture business," Wagner said. "What happened to her, that was like striking a match."

"I'm just glad I divorced you before I found out what a heel you really are."

— Miriam Halsworth (Claudette)to Hugh Halsworth (Macdonald Carey)

"Who wouldn't want to meet a man who has millions who isn't even bald?"

— Joyce Mannering (Monroe) to Hugh Halsworth (Macdonald Carey)

"Who Cares If It's Legal as Long as It's ...Tempting Virile Tantalizing Smooth Wow!"

— Tagline

Opposite page: Jerry and Hugh have a heart-to-heart talk. Top: Joyce wins big at cards. Bottom: Not even a locked door can keep Hugh away from Miriam.

CLASH BY NIGHT (1952)

RKO RADIO PICTURES
DIRECTOR: FRITZ LANG
SCREENPLAY: ALFRED HAYES
BASED ON THE PLAY BY CLIFFORD ODETS
PRINCIPAL CAST: BARBARA STANWYCK (MAE DOYLE D'AMATO), PAUL
DOUGLAS (JERRY D'AMATO), ROBERT RYAN (EARL PFEIFFER), MARILYN
MONROE (PEGGY) AND KEITH ANDES (JOE DOYLE)

Marilyn Monroe was just three years away from becoming the biggest star in movies when she appeared in Fritz Lang's *Clash by Night*, her first dramatic role and a giant step forward in her fledgling career. The chance to play opposite the great Barbara Stanwyck, under the guidance of a renowned filmmaker, was the type of break that every up-and-coming actress dreams about. But Monroe was much more than just another pretty, ambitious starlet and *Clash by Night* was her chance to prove it — to audiences and to herself.

Filmed on location in the fishing village of Monterey, California, *Clash by Night* centers on the character of Mae Doyle (Stanwyck), who returns to her hometown after a disappointing stint in New York City, and begins to build a better life by avoiding the mistakes of her past. She marries a local fisherman, Jerry D'Amato (Paul Douglas), a good-natured lout who barely interests her, but soon finds herself drawn to his crude, hard-edged

Top: Factory worker Peggy (Monroe) wakes up to another day on cannery row. Bottom: Joe Doyle (Keith Andes) with his girlfriend Peggy.

friend Earl (Robert Ryan), a projectionist at the local movie house who shares her jaded view of life and of love. Mae's brother Joe (Keith Andes) works on the fishing boats, and his young cannery row girlfriend, Peggy (Marilyn Monroe), becomes Mae's friend and counterpoint — a bubbly optimist who represents the hopes Mae once held about how wonderful life could be. Watching Peggy's relationship with Joe become increasingly abusive, and fighting off Earl's aggressive advances, Mae begins to wonder if she can ever escape cruelty, or if it's simply the way her life was always supposed to be.

With a career that stretched all the way back to the silent film era, director Lang brought to *Clash by Night* an artistic eye for composition and camera movement, and a remarkable ability to set the mood and advance the story with images alone. That talent added depth to many of his best-known films, including the futuristic epic *Metropolis* (1927) and the chilling thriller *M* (1931), and it adds to the impact of *Clash by Night* as well. Rather than speed the story along, he uses silent close-ups of his actors, adding to the anger and intensity shown by Ryan and Douglas, the weariness conveyed by Stanwyck, and the sweet sadness in Monroe's eyes.

Lang was notoriously demanding with actors, and he had little patience for Monroe's inability to remember her lines. She "flopped constantly," he complained later, and created distractions by secretly keeping her acting coach on the set, and taking her

Top: Home from New York, Mae Doyle (Barbara Stanwyck) befriends her younger brother's girlfriend, Peggy. Bottom: Mae is unsure about her feelings for Jerry (Paul Douglas), even as he professes his love.

The ruggedly handsome Earl (Robert Ryan) catches Peggy's eye. Opposite page: Joe seethes as Peggy chats up another man.

cues from the coach, rather than Lang. But the media attention Monroe brought to the production was of little concern to Lang, who wasn't inclined to judge her for the choices she made off the set, no matter how excited reporters seemed to be by the curvaceous starlet. In particular, the press had become very interested in Monroe because of a calendar she had posed nude for in the 1940s that suddenly surfaced just as shooting for *Clash by Night* began. Reporters swarmed around the production, ignoring established star Barbara Stanwyck to snap pictures of "that girl," as Lang recalled in a 1965 interview with director/film historian Peter Bogdanovich.

Stanwyck, who had been in more than 60 films by the time she made *Clash by Night*, understood that Monroe was an emerging star, and wasn't threatened by the attention being paid to the younger, inexperienced supporting player. In fact, when RKO decided to capitalize on Monroe's growing fame by giving her above-the-title billing, Stanwyck supported the studio's decision (the other cast members grumbled). Famously friendly and open on the set, Stanwyck genuinely liked Monroe and offered a sympathetic ear when the insecure 26-year-old actress worried that the media attention undermined her dramatic credibility in *Clash by Night*. The actresses' offscreen rapport comes through in their scenes together, enhancing both of their performances.

As fond as she was of Monroe, Stanwyck nevertheless grew tired of her co-star's lack of professionalism. In a 1965 interview with the *Toronto Telegram*, Stanwyck told the reporter that Monroe "couldn't get out of her own way. She wasn't disciplined, and she was often late, but she didn't do it viciously, and there was a sort of magic about her which we all recognized at once."

Indeed, Lang makes the most of Monroe's uncanny affinity with the camera in *Clash by Night*. He films her in long takes, giving Monroe the opportunity to show what she can do when given fine material and surrounded by seasoned co-stars. The result is one of her most captivating performances; even when her character

"Home is where you come when you run out of places."

— Mae (Barbara Stanwyck) to Peggy (Monroe)

does little more than stand to one side, Monroe holds the viewer's gaze. Reviewing *Clash by Night* for the *New York World-Telegram & Sun*, Alton Cook called Monroe "a forceful actress [and] a gifted new star, worthy of all that fantastic press agentry. Her role here is not very big, but she makes it dominant." Four decades later, Bogdanovich raved that "Monroe never makes a wrong move [in *Clash by Night*]. It's amazing. Even though she's the least accomplished actress. It's amazing how luminous and touching she is in everything she did in her short career."

Whereas Monroe and Stanwyck received excellent notices for *Clash by Night*, critics were less enthusiastic about Lang's adaptation of Clifford Odets'

"Whattya want, Joe? My life's history? Here it is in four words: Big ideas, small results."

— Mae (Barbara Stanwyck) to Joe (Keith Andes)

1941 drama, which had closed on Broadway after just 49 performances. *Variety* dubbed it "a rather aimless drama of lust and passion." Viewed today, *Clash by Night* is vintage Lang: a gripping, moodily effective noir with crackling, stylized dialogue.

After her small supporting roles in *The Asphalt Jungle* (1950) and *All About Eve* (1950), *Clash by Night* accelerated Monroe's rise. Lighter roles would follow, but her work with Lang established her as a formidable talent who

Opposite page: Alone with Earl, Mae can barely hide her disgust. Bottom: A drunken Peggy embarrasses herself at Mae and Jerry's wedding reception.

could be both engaging and believable in a dramatic film. It led to her first leading part in a dramatic feature film, as the psychotic babysitter in *Don't Bother to Knock* (1952), but more importantly it sent a message to filmgoers and the film industry in general: With "that girl" in *Clash by Night*, a new force in motion pictures had arrived.

"I never thought I'd like a guy who pushed me around."

— Peggy (Monroe) to Mae (Barbara Stanwyck)

Opposite page: Earl confesses his love as Mae fights her feelings. Top: Mae admits to her husband, Jerry, that she's fallen in love with Earl. Bottom: Joe gives Peggy an ultimatum about their relationship.

WE'RE NOT MARRIED (1952)

TWENTIETH CENTURY FOX

DIRECTOR: EDMUND GOULDING

SCREENPLAY: NUNNALLY JOHNSON AND DWIGHT TAYLOR

PRINCIPAL CAST: GINGER ROGERS (RAMONA GLADWYN), FRED ALLEN (STEVE GLADWYN), MARILYN MONROE (ANNABEL JONES NORRIS), DAVID WAYNE (JEFF NORRIS), DUFFY (JAMES GLEASON), VICTOR MOORE (MELVIN BUSH), EVE ARDEN (KATIE WOODRUFF), PAUL DOUGLAS (HECTOR WOODRUFF), EDDIE BRACKEN (WILLIE FISHER), MITZI GAYNOR (PATSY REYNOLDS FISHER), LOUIS CALHERN (FREDDIE MELROSE) AND ZSA ZSA GABOR (EVE MELROSE)

Holding up a mirror to the post–World War II era of suburbia, spiking marriage rates and the "baby boom," the romantic comedy *We're Not Married* wittily reflects the country's embrace of domesticity, circa 1952. The subject of matrimony — holy or otherwise — provides ample comic material for Edmund Goulding's film, which shrewdly capitalized on the growing box office appeal of Monroe, then poised on the brink of superstardom.

Written by Academy Award nominee Nunnally Johnson (*The Grapes of Wrath*) and Dwight Taylor, *We're Not Married* takes a single premise and spins five comedic possibilities. A doddering justice of the peace (Victor Moore), newly appointed and unsure of the rules, begins to marry couples before he's officially sworn in. Several years later, a government office notices the mistake. To avoid scandal, it's decided that an official notice must be

Top: Justice of the Peace Melvin Bush (Victor Moore) prepares to perform his first wedding service, with a little help from the bride and groom (Ginger Rogers and Fred Allen). Bottom: The Gladwyns tolerate each other just long enough to perform their radio show.

sent to five couples, who can then remedy the situation or ignore it as they choose.

The first of the five scenarios features the film's biggest stars, Ginger Rogers and Fred Allen, as Ramona and Steve Gladwyn, a miserable couple who perform as the "Glad Gladwyns" on a popular "Mr. and Mrs." radio show. Married only for appearances and profit, they shuffle past each other wordlessly at home but turn absurdly gracious when they're on the air.

Next are Jeff Norris (David Wayne) and his wife, Annabel (Monroe), an ambitious beauty queen who wins the title of Mrs. Mississippi, only to learn that it's the single contestants in the Miss America pageants who are getting all the sponsorship dollars.

In the third segment, Eve Arden and Paul Douglas play Katie and Hector Woodruff, a couple so mired in dull domestic routine that when Hector receives his official notice of non-marriage, he seriously considers whether he was better off in his swinging bachelor days.

The focus switches to tycoon Freddy Melrose (Louis Calhern) and his beautiful, gold-digging wife, Eve (Zsa Zsa Gabor), in the fourth segment of *We're Not Married*. And in the fifth and final segment, Eddie Bracken and Mitzi Gaynor portray Willie and Patsy Fisher, a young couple with a baby on the way, who race to remarry before the army ships Willie overseas.

Top: Annabel Jones Norris (Monroe) wins the Mrs. Mississippi Bathing Beauty Contest. Bottom: Time is running out for Willie Fisher (Eddie Bracken), who's anxious to tie the knot.

Great comic performances elevate the simple setups in *We're Not Married* and keep the stories fun and lively, even in their most cynical moments. As the "Mrs." half of the radio show arrangement, Ginger Rogers offers up the charm and wit that enlivened so many scenes between dance numbers earlier in her career. Fred Allen, a popular radio comedian of the 1940s, takes misery to new lows and, when the "Glad Gladwyns" mics go on, takes insincerity to hilarious highs. In her role as a bored housewife, Eve Arden delivers her lines with the sardonic deadpan wit that is her comic trademark. Zsa Zsa Gabor, famous for her love of opulence, has fun spoofing her image as a gold digger. And the versatile Mitzi Gaynor plays the straight woman to Eddie Bracken, the vaudeville-trained actor and *Our Gang* alumnus who brings *We're Not Married* to its comedic acme, as well as its sentimental finale.

"That little girl — wasn't she cute? You remember how she blushed about everything?"

— Justice of the Peace Melvin Bush (Victor Moore) remembering Annabel Jones Norris (Monroe)

Monroe also played to her strengths — at least, as far as the studio was concerned. With Monroe under contract to Twentieth Century Fox, studio head Darryl Zanuck was determined to cash in on her rising popularity by putting her in undemanding roles that showed her physically in the best possible light. Monroe brings to her character a bubbly enthusiasm — for her career, husband and baby — that is delightful and far from salacious, but the film's screenwriter, Nunnally Johnson, later discounted her efforts by claiming that the role of Annabel Jones Norris was created *only* to show Monroe in bathing suits.

Off screen, Monroe's life was anything but domestic. While *We're Not Married* was in preproduction, she met baseball superstar Joe DiMaggio, 12 years her senior, and within a month the two were dating steadily. DiMaggio, who had become interested in Monroe after seeing a photograph of her posing in a short-skirted baseball outfit, had little interest in the film industry, and Monroe knew nothing about baseball and had never attended a game. DiMaggio, recently retired from sports, believed women should be modest, and encouraged Monroe to be wary of the press and to settle down and raise a family. Monroe was tirelessly ambitious and showed no inclination to slow down just as she was taking off. But despite their differences, the relationship grew stronger as Monroe's career accelerated and as she deftly handled press attention that would have devastated a less confident star.

Shortly after DiMaggio and Monroe began dating, a nude photograph of her from years

Opposite page: Temporarily unmarried, Annabel joins other single women in the Miss Mississippi competition. Top: The bickering Woodruffs (Eve Arden and Paul Douglas) head toward another miserable night at home. Bottom: After learning that his marriage was never legally binding, Hector Woodruff dreams about being single once again.

Top: Eve Melrose (Zsa Zsa Gabor) informs husband Freddie (Louis Calhern) that she's planned a romantic evening for the two of them. Bottom: Freddie Melrose learns that Eve and her divorce lawyer (Paul Stewart) will clean out his fortune. Opposite page: With his wife-to-be Patsy (Mitzi Gaynor) standing by, Willie Fisher (Eddie Bracken) begs a justice of the peace for a quickie wedding before his ship leaves port.

earlier was republished on a 1952 calendar, and the press department at her studio was alarmed and unsure of how to handle the situation. Monroe seemed to know best: she told a UPI reporter that she had posed for the photo when she was young and needed money, the photographer was professional and "nice," and that she was completely unashamed of the result. The story was picked up by wire services, newspapers and magazines across the country. Three weeks later she was on the cover of *Life* magazine, with the caption, "Marilyn Monroe: The Talk of Hollywood."

We're Not Married boosted Monroe's career as well, furthering her reputation as a skilled comedic actress. The film proved irresistible, even to the habitual

"You have been scratched. You are now the ex-Mrs. Mississippi."

— Jeff Norris (David Wayne) to Annabel Jones Norris (Monroe)

curmudgeon Bosley Crowther, who reviewed it for the *New York Times:* "The idea itself is not reflective of the highest range of pure creative wit," he sniffed, "and the possibilities for bad humor and even worse taste are broad. But it must be said for Mr. Johnson and Mr. Goulding that they cut their capers well and came forth with a tailored entertainment that is one of the snappiest of the year."

The role of Annabel Jones Norris in *We're Not Married* was written specifically for Monroe. Opposite page: Duffy's plans for Annabel win Jeff's approval.

"We're just getting started with Mrs. America. We gotta hustle for everything we get."

— Duffy (James Gleason) to Jeff and Annabel Norris (David Wayne and Monroe)

Don't Bother to Knock (1952)

Twentieth Century Fox

Director: Roy Ward Baker

Screenplay: Daniel Taradash

Based on the novel "Mischief" by Charlotte Armstrong

Principal Cast: Richard Widmark (Jed Towers), Marilyn Monroe (Nell Forbes), Anne Bancroft (Lyn Leslie), Donna Corcoran (Bunny Jones), Jeanne Cagney (Rochelle), Lurene Tuttle (Mrs. Jones), Elisha Cook Jr. (Eddie Forbes), Jim Backus (Peter Jones), Verna Felton (Mrs. Ballew) and Don Bleddoe (Mr. Ballew)

It was to be her juiciest role yet, a make-or-break opportunity to prove she was more than just a voluptuous piece of eye candy. With *Don't Bother to Knock*, Monroe hoped she could move beyond playing decorative roles as dizzy blondes and establish herself as a capable and serious actress. She had received fine notices for work in *Clash by Night* (1952), but Barbara Stanwyck had played the lead role in Fritz Lang's adaptation of Clifford Odets' play. *Don't Bother to Knock* would give Monroe her first major dramatic role in a studio film.

Directed by British filmmaker Roy Ward Baker, *Don't Bother to Knock* is a taut and unsettling adaptation of mystery writer Charlotte Armstrong's 1951 novel *Mischief*, first serialized in *Good Housekeeping*. Playing a role originally intended for Dorothy McGuire, Monroe delivers a breakthrough performance as Nell Forbes, a lonely and psychologically disturbed babysitter who

Top: Monroe toned down the glamour to play the troubled Nell Forbes in *Don't Bother to Knock*. Bottom: An anxious Nell prepares to meet Bunny, the little girl she's babysitting.

becomes fatefully entangled with airline pilot Jed Towers (Richard Widmark).

Written for the screen by Daniel Taradash, *Don't Bother to Knock* takes place in New York's McKinley Hotel, where lounge singer Lyn Lesley (Anne Bancroft, in her feature film debut) has decided to break up with Jed, her boyfriend of six months. Furious and hurt at being dumped, Jed attempts to rebound with Nell, the shy niece of the McKinley hotel's elevator operator, Eddie Forbes (Elisha Cook Jr.). After catching a glimpse of her through his hotel room window, Jed impulsively calls the beautiful young woman, who's babysitting Bunny (Donna Corcoran), the young daughter of hotel guests. It's a phone call he'll soon regret making, for Nell reveals herself to be psychologically fragile and incapable of distinguishing between fantasy and reality. When Bunny sleepily interrupts their date, Nell angrily turns on the little girl and shakes her. Her violent outburst drives Jed back to Lyn — yet he's forced to return when Nell terrorizes Bunny and threatens to commit suicide.

Although Monroe reportedly considered *Don't Bother to Knock* one of her finest dramatic performances, she nevertheless struggled with anxiety throughout the filming. Under tremendous pressure to prove herself, especially to Fox studio chief Darryl F. Zanuck, Monroe didn't receive much guidance from Baker, according to Susan Doll's 2007 article "Marilyn Monroe's Early Career" for the website HowStuffWorks.com. A journeyman filmmaker best remembered for *A Night to*

Top: Nell tries on the jewelry of Bunny's mother.
Bottom: Eddie (Elisha Cook Jr.) reprimands his oblivious niece for trying on guest's jewelry and clothing.

Nell gets a phone call from Jed Towers (Richard Widmark, visible in window).

Remember (1958) and a string of Hammer horror films, Baker failed to help Monroe flesh out her character's psychological back story to the actress' satisfaction. Not that Monroe was at a loss for inspiration, given her own troubled childhood and visits to her mother in mental institutions. Nor did Monroe relish the prospect of working on a very tight shooting schedule, which often allowed only one take per scene.

In spite of these challenges, Monroe seemed to get on well with the cast. Co-star Richard Widmark, unsure about her at first, eventually was in awe: "We had a hell of a time getting her out of the dressing room and on to the set. At first we thought she'd never get anything right…. But something happened between the lens and the film, and when we looked at the rushes she had the rest of us knocked off the screen!"

And the results were, indeed, mesmerizing. The *New York Daily News* proclaimed Monroe "as more than a sexy dame. She has good dramatic promise. She is a

"Sometimes I feel strong inside but I have to reach in and pull it up. It isn't easy. Nothing's easy. But you go on."

— Monroe (reacting to the acclaim from her performance in her first starring role)

provocative woman even in the drab costume of a poor hireling. She is what the movies need. A few more like her and the industry would thrive." *The Motion Picture Tribune* asserted: "It proves conclusively that she is the kind of big new star for which exhibitors are always asking."

Though some critics remained wary of her dramatic abilities in the face of her undeniably stunning physicality, the *New York Post*'s critic wrote "In *Don't Bother to Knock*…they've thrown Marilyn Monroe into the deep dramatic waters, sink or swim, and while she doesn't really do either, you might say that she floats. With that figure, what else can she do?" But it was clear she had made a palpable impact within the industry and upon the moviegoing public in her first starring role.

Today *Don't Bother to Knock* is regarded as something of a curio. Looking back screenwriter Daniel Taradash believed "if they had spent more money…they might have had something. As it stands now, it is an oddity—a cult film." But the entire concoction still holds up as a compelling amalgam of noir, love story, character study and suspense thriller. And Monroe's performance gleams, haunts and disturbs. The totality of her achievement in *Don't Bother to Knock* is summed up in director

Jed catches Nell in a lie.

63

"I really reacted to her. She moved me so that tears came to my eyes. Believe me, such moments happened rarely, if ever again, in the early things I was doing."

— Anne Bancroft on working with Monroe

Top: Nell begins to unravel. Bottom: Nell teeters on the brink of madness. Opposite page: Monroe was proud of her performance in *Don't Bother to Knock*.

John Logan's observation: "Marilyn is as near genius as any actress I ever knew…. She is the most completely realized actress since Garbo. Watch her work. In any film. How rarely she has to use words. How much she does with here eyes, her lips, with slight, almost accidental gestures. Monroe is pure cinema."

"You're a gal with a lot of variations…silk on one side and sandpaper on the other."

— Jed Towers (Richard Widmark) to Nell (Monroe)

MONKEY BUSINESS (1952)

TWENTIETH CENTURY FOX

DIRECTOR: HOWARD HAWKS

SCREENPLAY: BEN HECHT, CHARLES LEDERER, I.A.L. DIAMOND

PRINCIPAL CAST: CARY GRANT (DR. BARNABY FULTON), GINGER ROGERS (EDWINA FULTON), CHARLES COBURN (MR. OLIVER OXLEY) AND MARILYN MONROE (MISS LOIS LAUREL)

Many years after making *Monkey Business*, director Howard Hawks confided to an interviewer that the film "was not as funny as it should have been." Given the pedigree of the film's cast and screenwriters — the latter a trio of Hollywood veterans, including Academy Award winner Ben Hecht — Hawks' disappointment with the final product is understandable. Yet while it's never as consistently clever or witty as Hawks' classic screwball comedies *Bringing Up Baby* (1938) and *His Girl Friday* (1940), *Monkey Business* is still one of the director's most engaging films, thanks in large part to the crackerjack performances by Cary Grant, Ginger Rogers, character actor Charles Coburn and willowy star-on-the-rise Marilyn Monroe. Although she only appears in a relatively few scenes, the fourth-billed Monroe makes the very most of her screen time in *Monkey Business*, which helped put the Fox contract player's career on the fast track. Two years after she wiggled her way around the laboratory beakers in

Top: Domestic bliss: Dr. Barnaby Fulton (Cary Grant) and his wife, Edwina (Ginger Rogers), at home. Bottom: Monroe at her dizzy best as Miss Laurel.

Hawks' 1952 comedy, Monroe would be the biggest sex symbol in America.

Ironically, Monroe's rising stardom came at a dear price for the fragile beauty. The more publicity she attracted, "the more frightened she became," according to Hawks, who would subsequently direct her in *Gentlemen Prefer Blondes* (1953). During the shooting of *Monkey Business*, she worried constantly that she wasn't attractive enough. At the same time, she was hospitalized with appendicitis just after filming began. Fearing that Hawks would replace her, she refused surgery. Doctors instead froze Monroe's appendix to buy her more time, and as soon as filming was completed, Monroe entered the hospital again and had it removed. For all her insecurities and anxieties, Monroe wasn't about to let anything, not even a serious medical condition, derail her dream of Hollywood stardom.

In *Monkey Business*, Monroe plays Miss Lois Laurel, the secretary to Mr. Oliver Oxly (Coburn), the head of Oxly Chemical Company. Oxly's chief research chemist is the absent-minded Dr. Barnaby Fulton (Grant), whose long-suffering wife, Edwina (Ginger Rogers), puts up with his inattentiveness because she knows he's a genius. Barnaby is working on a revitalization formula that his boss is already beginning to market as "B-4," a fountain-of-youth drug. Isolating the chemical compounds has yielded promising results; what Barnaby must do now is mix them in the right combination to produce a miracle elixir.

Top: Barnaby inspects Miss Laurel's "acetates."
Bottom: Mr. Oxly (Charles Coburn) gives Miss Laurel her latest assignment.

A rejuvenated Barnaby takes Miss Laurel for a spin.

In true screwball comedy fashion, an escaped laboratory chimpanzee mixes the right combination of chemicals and dumps the potion in the water cooler. A few swigs later, Barnaby is acting like an 18-year-old; he buys some snazzy new threads and whisks Miss Laurel away for a joy ride in his brand spanking new hot rod. They spend the rest of the afternoon roller skating and swimming at a pool, where all eyes are riveted on her. Not to be outdone, Edwina drinks from the tainted water cooler and undergoes a similar rejuvenation, but everything goes haywire when she and Barnaby drink too much from the miracle elixir and start acting like bratty children.

Grant and Rogers may receive top billing for *Monkey Business*, but it's Monroe who holds the screen with her voluptuous beauty. Of course, Hawks accentuates the starlet's physical charms by frequently shooting her in profile or focusing on her shapely legs. In one scene, Miss Laurel says to Barnaby, "I'm glad we have a moment. I have something to show you," before she raises her skirt to reveal she's wearing the acetate stockings he designed.

"Charles Coburn as a drug manufacturer, Marilyn Monroe as his secretary and many more throw themselves into the nonsense with a fine and abandoned will."

— Bosley Crowther, the *New York Times*

What ultimately makes Monroe's *Monkey Business* character irresistible, however, is the star's magical elixir of sex appeal, sweetness and comic flair. When Barnaby remarks that she's in the office early, Monroe gives Miss Laurel's reply her inimitable combination of breathlessness and naiveté: "Oh, yes, Mr. Oxly's been complaining about my punctuation, so I'm careful to get here before nine." Later, when told by Mr. Oxly that he wants her to go to every Ford agency in town and find Dr. Fulton, she replies, "But Mr. Oxly, which shall I do first?"

A box office hit, *Monkey Business* didn't wow the critics, who rightly complained that it paled in comparison to Hawks' earlier films. In his *New York Times* review, Bosley Crowther wrote that "it bubbles and throws off a lot of surprise so long as its single gag is running more or less up-hill," but turns "just a little dull" at other times. Indeed, except for those sequences when Dr. Fulton, his wife, or the Oxly bunch are under the effects of the youth serum and behaving quite like the chimpanzee, *Monkey Business* lacks the razor-sharp comic timing and narrative drive that propels both *Bringing Up Baby* and *His Girl Friday*.

If American critics were lukewarm about *Monkey Business*, Hawks' film was hailed as a masterpiece by French critic and filmmaker Jacques Rivette, a core member of the "French New Wave," in a 1953 essay for the intellectual film journal *Cahier du Cinema*. Equal parts mash note and heady theoretical dissertation, Rivette's "The Genius of Howard Hawks" opening line brooks no dissent:

"The evidence on the screen is the proof of Howard Hawks's genius: you only have to watch *Monkey Business* to know that it is a brilliant film.

Top: Dr. Fulton decides to become his own guinea pig. Bottom: Miss Laurel dazzles poolside.

"[*Monkey Business*] presented an opportunity for Hawks to figure out how Marilyn should be used. When he knew that, he'd have the formula that would enable Marilyn to become a star."

— Barbara Leaming, *Marilyn Monroe*

Top: Edwina has taken a swig of the youth serum, with comically disastrous results. Bottom: Oxly and Miss Laurel don't know what to make of the change in Edwina. Opposite page: The absent-minded professor: Barnaby hard at work in his lab.

Some people refuse to admit this, however; they refuse to be satisfied by proof. There can't be any other reason why they don't recognize it."

As for Monroe, Rivette praises her "sweet stupidity" as Miss Laurel and goes on to describe her as "that monster of femininity whom the costume designer nearly deformed" (!) — certainly the most backhanded compliment ever paid the screen's greatest sex symbol.

"Marilyn Monroe's sex appeal is played up for all it's worth (and that's not inconsiderable)."

— *Variety* film review

PART 2

1953-1959

Marilyn Monroe: 1953-1959

Marilyn Monroe's early years in Hollywood were marked by an ability to create tremendous publicity, but an inability to break out as a major star. That all changed in 1953 when she released not one, not two, but three hit films in a row: *Niagara*, *Gentlemen Prefer Blondes* and *How to Marry a Millionaire*. Suddenly, Monroe was in the center of the cultural radar. She was a newly minted star, she was dating one of America's sports heroes, Joe DiMaggio, and in December of that year, she was the cover girl for Hugh Hefner's new magazine, *Playboy*. As "Sweetheart of the Month," Monroe also graced the centerfold with her notorious nude calendar shot.

Riding high on a wave of fame and success, Monroe expected respect from her employers at Twentieth Century Fox. The studio responded by casting her in *River of No Return* (1954) — a film which Monroe starred in, but publicly scorned. In January of 1954, she refused to appear in the next film the studio selected for her and she was suspended.

Monroe's Leading Men, 1953-1959

Joseph Cotten
Niagara (1953)

By the time he portrayed Monroe's husband in *Niagara*, Cotten was beginning his shift from leading man to character actor. A charter member of Orson Welles' Mercury Theatre company, Cotten starred in two of Welles' most acclaimed films: *Citizen Kane* (1941) and *The Magnificent Ambersons* (1942). He also won praise for his chilling performance in Alfred Hitchcock's *Shadow of a Doubt* (1943).

Tony Curtis
Some Like It Hot (1959)

Ten years after his 1949 affair with Monroe, Curtis wooed her on-screen in Billy Wilder's comic masterpiece. *Some Like It Hot* would cap a remarkable two-year run for the Bronx native, born Bernard Schwartz, who had silenced critics with his triumphant performances in *Sweet Smell of Success* (1957) and *The Defiant Ones* (1958); the latter film earned Curtis an Academy Award nomination for Best Actor.

Tom Ewell
The Seven Year Itch (1955)

Reprising his Tony Award-winning role opposite Monroe in *The Seven Year Itch*, the veteran stage actor won a Golden Globe for his performance. Although Ewell worked steadily in film and television until the 1980s, most notably on the television series *Baretta*, he mostly played supporting roles, save for *The Girl Can't Help It* (1956), co-starring Jayne Mansfield.

> "Standing in the snowfall facing these yelling soldiers, I felt for the first time in my life no fear of anything. I felt only happy."
>
> — Monroe on performing for U.S. troops in Korea

Undaunted, Monroe left Hollywood to marry DiMaggio. While on their honeymoon in Japan, an American general invited Monroe to come to Korea to entertain U.S. troops. Monroe accepted and thus began a four-day, ten-performance engagement that she would later describe as one of the major highlights of her career. Although it was freezing cold, Monroe wore only a low-cut dress as she sang and joked for the soldiers. Delivering come-hither lines like, "You fellas are always whistling at sweater girls. Well, take away their sweaters and what have they got?" Monroe received thunderous applause and wolf whistles from the troops.

Back in the United States, Monroe hammered out a new agreement with Fox. She would do *There's No Business Like Show Business* (1954) in exchange for the lead role in *The Seven Year Itch*. During the filming of this latter film, in October of 1954, Monroe announced that her marriage to Joe DiMaggio was over. In need of a retreat from Hollywood and heartbreak, Monroe moved to New York in December 1954. The next month, Fox suspended Monroe again when she refused to appear in *How to Be Very, Very Popular* (1955).

JACK LEMMON
Some Like It Hot (1959)

One of the most versatile and admired stars in Hollywood history, Lemmon received the second of his eight Academy Award nominations for his hilarious performance in *Some Like It Hot*. He had previously won Best Supporting Actor for *Mister Roberts* (1955), and would later take the Best Actor statuette for *Save the Tiger* (1973). *Some Like It Hot* is one of seven films Lemmon made with director Billy Wilder: the others are *The Apartment* (1960), *Irma La Douce* (1963), *The Fortune Cookie* (1966), *Avanti!* (1972), *The Front Page* (1974) and *Buddy Buddy* (1981).

ROBERT MITCHUM
River of No Return (1954)

The sleepy-eyed film noir icon had little patience for Monroe's reliance on controlling drama coach Natasha Lytess while filming *River of No Return* in the Canadian Rockies. The Otto Preminger film was one of two westerns Mitchum made in 1954, the other being William Wellman's *Track of the Cat*. The following year, Mitchum would give one of his all-time greatest performances as the psychotic preacher in Charles Laughton's haunting masterpiece, *The Night of the Hunter* (1955).

LAURENCE OLIVIER
The Prince and the Showgirl (1957)

A towering figure in British stage and cinema, Olivier was the antithesis of Monroe: a classically trained actor who excelled at bringing Shakespeare's *Henry V* (1946), *Hamlet* (1948) and *Richard III* (1956) to the screen. Olivier also found great success in Hollywood, starring in *Wuthering Heights* (1939), *Rebecca* (1940) and *Marathon Man* (1976). Although Monroe reportedly enraged Olivier with her chronic tardiness and unprofessional behavior, he later conceded that she was a uniquely gifted actress.

Monroe's goal in New York was to grow as a person and as an actress. To this end, she began classes at Lee Strasberg's Actors Studio. Strasberg was the creator of The Method, an approach to acting based on the teachings of the Russian acting teacher Konstantin Stanislavsky. The Method instructs actors to use their own personal memories and emotions to explore and inhabit the characters they play. Monroe embraced this approach wholeheartedly and began psychoanalysis to improve her technique. During this time, she met the legendary playwright Arthur Miller. Although he was married at the time, the two began a romance.

Meanwhile in Hollywood, Fox wasn't sure if Monroe would ever return and they joined the quest with other studios to find "the next Monroe." Universal's answer was Mamie Van Doren. A former model, Van Doren gained a following with *The Second Greatest Sex* (1955) and *Running Wild* (1955), but never broke out of B-movie fare. Columbia put forth Kim Novak. She appeared in *Pushover* and *Phffft* in 1954, but gained more serious attention for her roles in *Picnic* (1955) and *Vertigo* (1958).

Donald O'Connor and Mitzi Gaynor with Monroe in *There's No Business Like Show Business* (1954).

"Why haven't I the right to grow and expand like everybody else?"

— Monroe, on her life in New York

Fox aggressively pushed Sheree North as their next Monroe. Indeed, North was cast in two movies that Monroe had rejected — *How to Be Very, Very Popular* (1955) and *The Lieutenant Wore Skirts* (1956). Neither film did well at the box office. The other actress Fox heavily promoted was Jayne Mansfield. Mansfield teamed with Monroe's *The Seven Year Itch* co-star Tom Ewell for *The Girl Can't Help It* (1956) and good-naturedly ribbed Monroe in *Will Success Spoil Rock Hunter?* (1957). Although Mansfield attracted a lot of publicity, Hollywood never viewed her as anything more than a camp sex symbol whose shtick wore out fast. Mansfield spent the remainder of her career appearing in exploitation films and dive nightclubs before dying in a horrific car accident in 1967.

Monroe was not oblivious to her imitators. She once said, "Sometimes I kid the fans. They say, 'Oh, you're Marilyn Monroe!' I say, 'Oh no, I'm Mamie Van Doren or Sheree North.'" Along with these American contenders, there was also Gina Lollobrigida, "Italy's Marilyn Monroe" and Brigitte Bardot, France's blonde bombshell. With all the competition, it was inevitable that Monroe would not get all the parts she desired. She wanted to play Adelaide in *Guys and Dolls* (1954),

"She represents to man something we all want in our unfulfilled dreams. A man, he's got to be dead not to be excited by her."

– Jean Negulesco, director of *How to Marry a Millionaire*

Monroe in *Niagara* (1953).

but Broadway star Vivian Blaine reprised her stage role on-screen. Another role she coveted was the title character in Elia Kazan's *Baby Doll* (1956), an adaptation of Tennessee Williams' *27 Wagons Full of Cotten*, yet she lost out to newcomer Carroll Baker. Finally, Monroe endured ridicule when she announced her desire to portray Grushenka in a film version of Dostoevsky's *The Brothers Karamazov;* Austrian actress Maria Schell eventually played the role in Richard Brooks' 1958 adaptation of the classic Russian novel, starring Yul Brynner.

When *The Seven Year Itch* was released in June of 1955, it became a box office hit and gave Monroe the leverage she needed to make Fox sign a contract that would give her more control over her career. The next film she chose to do was *Bus Stop* (1956), in which she first incorporated her Method techniques. As soon as filming completed, Monroe married Arthur Miller and headed off to London to begin work with Laurence Olivier in *The Prince and the Showgirl* (1957).

Late in 1957, Billy Wilder sent Monroe a synopsis of *Some Like It Hot* (1959).

"She can call up emotionally what is required for a scene. Her range is infinite."

– Lee Strasberg, director of The Actors Studio

Monroe and David Wayne in *How to Marry a Millionaire* (1953).

Initially, she was reluctant to play a supporting role, but Miller convinced her to do it. As it turned out, *Some Like It Hot* delivered Monroe her most successful film ever and a Golden Globe for Best Actress-Musical or Comedy. It was a fitting exclamation point to a decade that had catapulted Marilyn Monroe from a starlet to an icon.

Monroe in *There's No Business Like Show Business* (1954).

"She has a certain indefinable magic that comes across, which no other actress in the business has."

– Billy Wilder, director of *The Seven Year Itch* and *Some Like It Hot*

NIAGARA (1953)

TWENTIETH CENTURY FOX

DIRECTOR: HENRY HATHAWAY

SCREENPLAY: CHARLES BRACKETT, RICHARD L. BREEN AND WALTER REISCH

PRINCIPAL CAST: MARILYN MONROE (ROSE LOOMIS), JOSEPH COTTEN (GEORGE LOOMIS), JEAN PETERS (POLLY CUTLER), CASEY ADAMS (RAY CUTLER), DENIS O'DEA (INSPECTOR STARKEY), RICHARD ALLAN (TED PATRICK), DON WILSON (MR. KETTERLING) AND LURENE TUTTLE (MRS. KETTERLING)

In veteran director Henry Hathaway's suspense drama *Niagara* (1953), two forces of nature command center stage: Niagara Falls and Marilyn Monroe, each exactingly showcased, packaged and presented to their best advantage in glorious Technicolor. As the unhappily married femme fatale Rose Loomis, Monroe easily upstages one of nature's most scenic wonders with her star-making performance. Directed with crisp efficiency by Hathaway, this torrid melodrama forever enshrined Monroe as the cinematic embodiment of sex — an image she would simultaneously embrace and rebel against in her subsequent film roles.

Filmed on location on the Canadian side of Niagara Falls, *Niagara* begins with a stunning shot of this popular tourist spot and scenic wonder. Two couples are on vacation: belated honeymooners Polly (Jean Peters, who replaced Monroe's *All About Eve* co-star Anne Baxter) and Ray Cutler (Casey Adams), and battle-fatigued Korean War veteran George Loomis (Joseph Cotten) and

Top: Monroe scorches the screen as femme fatale Rose Loomis in *Niagara*. Bottom: Ted (Richard Allan) and Rose share an illicit kiss.

his bored, beautiful wife, Rose (Monroe). While George sleeps, Rose confides to the Cutlers that he spent some time in a military psychiatric hospital. Later, Polly spots Rose in an illicit embrace with her lover, Ted Patrick (Richard Allan).

That evening at the hotel, Rose asks a group of teenagers dancing in the courtyard to play her favorite song, "Kiss," which she in turn seductively sings. When George hears the song, he storms out of his room, grabs the record from the turntable and smashes it. Panicking, Rose calls her lover and tells him that it's time to put their plan to kill George into action. When their scheme suddenly goes awry, however, Rose winds up in a hospital and is sedated for hysteria.

After discovering his wife's plan, George decides to exact his revenge. In desperation Rose escapes from the hospital and tries to make it to the American side of the falls, but George relentlessly pursues her to the top of a bell tower, setting the stage for *Niagara's* spectacular finale.

While *Niagara* occasionally loses its narrative momentum, particularly whenever Monroe's off screen, it's nevertheless skillfully directed by Hathaway, who'd won acclaim for his noir crime dramas *Kiss of Death* (1947) and *Call Northside 777* (1948). There are extended, wordless sequences in *Niagara* that bear favorable comparison to the work of Alfred Hitchcock. Indeed, the bell tower sequence and Hathaway's bell

Top: Monroe was 27 years old when *Niagara* cemented her stardom. Bottom: "Light me up, too, Georgie!" Rose (Monroe) teases her husband (Joseph Cotten).

carillon montages call to mind Hitchock's masterpiece, *Vertigo* (1958). Although Hitchcock reportedly considered Monroe one of the only genuine female film stars in Hollywood (the others being Ingrid Bergman and Elizabeth Taylor), they never made a film together — though he was on Monroe's personally compiled 1955 list of approved directors.

The filming of *Niagara* lasted two months and was completed in July of 1952. When it was later released on January 21, 1953, the *New York Times'* A. H. Weiler raved about the film as a showcase for Monroe: "Obviously ignoring the idea that there are Seven Wonders of the World, Twentieth Century Fox has discovered two more and enhanced them with Technicolor in *Niagara*.... For the producers are making full use of both the grandeur of the Falls and its adjacent areas as well as the grandeur that is Marilyn Monroe.... And they have illustrated pretty concretely that she can be seductive — even when she walks. As has been noted…the Falls and Miss Monroe are something to see."

Rose performing her seductive rendition of "Kiss."

"I think cheesecake helps call attention to you. Then you can follow through and prove yourself."

— Monroe, on modeling

That Monroe had reduced the veteran *New York Times* critic to a fawning schoolboy is understandable. *Niagara* cinematographer Joseph MacDonald captures "the grandeur that is Marilyn Monroe" in blazingly red hot images of the star, most notably her first appearance on-screen: smoking in bed, a sheet barely concealing her nude form. Later, she appears in one of her most unforgettable costumes: a scorching, low-cut magenta dress that screen husband Cotten describes as "cut down so low in front you can see her kneecaps." Whether Monroe's seductively crooning the Lionel Newman and Haven Gillespie song "Kiss" or making her famed, hip-swiveling 116-foot walk away from the camera in a skintight black dress, she comes across as one of the most alluring femme fatales in screen history, as provocative as Marlene Dietrich during her period as Josef Von Sternberg's muse. She dominates *Niagara,* possessing every frame in a riveting performance largely free of the mannerisms she displayed in her previous role as the psychotic babysitter in *Don't Bother to Knock* (1952). It's no wonder that Hathaway raved about

"Marilyn Monroe and Niagara — a raging torrent of emotion that even nature can't control!"

— *Niagara* tagline

Rose plotting the perfect crime.

83

"Mrs. Loomis! If I hear that name once more I'll start yelling myself. No wonder it got you. We wait three years for a honeymoon, then spend it with a couple of spooks."

— Casey Adams (Ray Cutler)

Top: Newlywed Polly Cutler (Jean Peters) suspects Rose is up to no good. Bottom: A drugged Rose, confined to her hospital bed. Opposite page: Rose's scheme begins to unravel.

Monroe's performance to Hollywood columnist Sidney Skolsky before *Niagara*'s release: "She's the best natural actress I've directed. And she's the greatest natural talent. Wait 'til you see her in this picture."

A box office smash, earning five times what it cost to make, *Niagara*'s bold depiction of sex, insanity and infidelity, coupled with Monroe's sizzling performance, qualify it as one of the actress' best movies.

"What lifts the film above the commonplace is its star, Marilyn Monroe."

— *Time* magazine

GENTLEMEN PREFER BLONDES (1953)

TWENTIETH CENTURY FOX

DIRECTOR: HOWARD HAWKS

SCREENPLAY: CHARLES LEDERER

BASED ON THE MUSICAL BY JOSEPH FIELDS AND ANITA LOOS

PRINCIPAL CAST: MARILYN MONROE (LORELEI LEE), JANE RUSSELL (DOROTHY SHAW), CHARLES COBURN (SIR FRANCIS "PIGGY" BEEKMAN), ELLIOTT REID (ERNIE MALONE) AND TOMMY NOONAN (GUS ESMOND)

When Broadway dancer Gwen Verdon was hired to coach the stars of *Gentlemen Prefer Blondes* for their dance numbers, she was asked to help take some of the "sex" out of Monroe's movements. As Monroe's performance in Howard Hawks' zestfully entertaining musical comedy demonstrates, however, taking the "sex" out of her persona may be like trying to take the "sweet" out of honey. *Gentlemen Prefer Blondes* gives Monroe's irresistible combination of sexuality, charm and humor perhaps one of its funniest and fullest expressions — and plenty of room to seduce generations of fans.

Based on the 1949 hit Broadway musical (which in turn had been adapted from Anita Loos' 1925 novella), *Gentlemen Prefer Blondes* follows the romantic misadventures of two showgirls, Lorelei Lee (Monroe) and Dorothy Shaw (Jane Russell), on a luxury cruise to France. The

Top: Lorelei Lee (Monroe) and Dorothy Shaw (Jane Russell) are just two "little girls from Little Rock" in the film's bouncy opening number. Bottom: Lorelei "shares some advice" on how a girl might get ahead in life, setting the stage for the hijinks to follow.

pairing plays as a kind of strategic fission of Mae West's earlier screen persona: Down-to-earth Dorothy wants to marry for love and tosses off one-liners as easily as others breathe. Blonde bombshell Lorelei wants nothing more than to marry a millionaire and all but flashes dollar signs every time she bats her eyes. In fact, she's managed to thoroughly bewitch the son of a tycoon — one mousy, straight-laced Gus Esmond Jr. (Tommy Noonan). Gus proposes to her on the eve of the cruise, but as so happens, the elder Esmond doesn't trust "that man-trap" Lorelei and sends private detective Ernie Malone (Elliott Reid) after her to ferret out any scandal aboard ship.

Malone swiftly gets more than he bargained for when he finds Lorelei cozying up to diamond-mine owner "Piggy" Beekman (Charles Coburn), in an effort to unburden him of a prized tiara. In the meantime, he's distracted by Dorothy's own brand of charm and finds himself falling in love with her. When Dorothy discovers him spying on Lorelei, however, she assumes his attentions have simply been a cynical means of getting closer to Lorelei and endeavors to pay him back for his ungentlemanly tactics.

Directed by Howard Hawks, the most versatile filmmaker of Hollywood's golden age, *Gentlemen Prefer Blondes* contrives a lightweight, tongue-in-cheek, confectionary showcase for Monroe and Russell, who shimmer and shimmy as brightly as Cartier gemstones. Their personas complement each other perfectly in

Top: Dorothy appraises Lorelei's latest gift as Gus (Tommy Noonan) watches. Bottom: The Olympic relay team sings backup for Dorothy.

Gus can't resist Lorelei's charms. Opposite page: Lovely in lavender.

Charles Lederer's witty screenplay. Lederer, who had previously written *His Girl Friday* (1940) and *Monkey Business* (1952) for Hawks, depicts Lorelei and Dorothy's friendship as a loyal sisterhood. Both Monroe and Russell find that "sweet spot" of generosity in their performances and allow the audience to revel in, rather than sneer at, their husband-chasing antics. Monroe is an especially artful and disarming ray of light. At turns coy and conniving, airheaded and knowing, Monroe finds the logic in Lorelei's gold-digging and never lets you dismiss her as just a "dumb blonde." Nor does Lorelei ever become jaded or cold. On the contrary, Monroe infuses the role with the warmth and playfulness that always bracketed her sensuality and endeared her to both men and women. But unlike her later roles, which seemed to take on a wounded innocence in need of a good hug, Lorelei is at the top of her alluring game: ever confident and in control.

Gentlemen Prefer Blondes was originally intended to be a vehicle for Betty Grable, who had been Twentieth Century Fox's top box office star for years. After the success of Monroe's *Niagara* (1953), though, the studio realized

"Don't you know that a man being rich is like a girl being pretty? You wouldn't marry a girl just because she's pretty, but my goodness, doesn't it help?"

— Lorelei Lee (Monroe)

they had a potential goldmine of their own in Monroe, who also came at a considerable bargain compared to Grable. Monroe reportedly earned only $18,000 for her part in *Gentlemen Prefer Blondes*, whereas Grable was earning an average of $150,000 per picture.

While casting Monroe may have been one of Twentieth Century Fox's wisest moves, it was no bargain for Hawks, who had suffered through Monroe's antics and chronic insecurities during the filming of *Monkey Business*, which featured her in a showy supporting role. On the *Gentlemen Prefer Blondes* shoot, Monroe again drove Hawks to distraction with her unprofessional behavior. She reportedly hid in her trailer, and, when finally coaxed out by Russell, demanded several retakes of her scenes. At one point the studio asked Hawks how production might be sped up, to which he retorted, "Replace Marilyn, rewrite the script and make it shorter, and get a new director."

Thankfully, only one of those "wonderful ideas" bore fruit. *Blondes* sails in at a

"I want you to find happiness and stop having fun."

– Lorelei Lee (Monroe)

breezy 91 minutes. Several proposed song-and-dance numbers, including "Down Boy," penned by Hoagy Carmichael and intended for Monroe, were eventually cut. In fitting irony, "Down Boy" was later handed to Grable, who sang it in *Three for the Show* (1955).

Erroneously dismissed by some critics as lowbrow entertainment, *Gentlemen Prefer Blondes* never pretends to be anything more than slightly giddy popcorn fare, a delicious romp. The humor remains light on its feet and ranges from witty wordplay to broad physical comedy, with perhaps one of the most memorable moments coming at the expense of Monroe's own hourglass assets. While the musical numbers might never achieve the greatness of an MGM classic, they are catchy and bouncy enough to hum long after the final fade-out.

Of course, the film's *pièce de résistance* is "Diamonds Are a Girl's Best Friend." Originally performed on stage by Carol Channing — whom Judy Holliday, once

"I can be smart when it's important, but most men don't like it."

— Lorelei Lee (Monroe), a line supposedly suggested by Monroe during shooting.

> "I always say a kiss on the hand might feel very good, but a diamond tiara lasts forever."
>
> — Lorelei Lee (Monroe)

Opposite page: Lorelei Lee "finding new places to wear diamonds." Top: Dorothy arm-in-arm with Ernie Malone (Elliot Reed), a detective hired to follow Lorelei. Bottom: Lorelei doesn't quite know what to make of her latest suitor, "Piggy"(Charles Coburn).

offered the role of Lorelei, thought should be the only performer to sing it — the number became a classic with Monroe's rendition. Re-created in stunning detail in Madonna's 1985 "Material Girl" video and since reimagined in Baz Luhrmann's *Moulin Rouge* (2001), July Styne and Leo Robin's song has transcended *Gentlemen Prefer Blondes* to become a pop culture icon. In 2004, "Diamonds Are a Girl's Best Friend" came in twelfth in the American Film Institute's ranking of the top 100 film songs of all time.

That "Diamonds Are a Girl's Best Friend" is forever identified with Monroe is no surprise. Like her, the musical number winks, plays and bounces with sensual allure: artful in its artlessness, seductive in its innocence and charming in its power. A cinematic gem, as enduring as Monroe.

"Well, whatever I am, I'm still the blonde."

— Monroe, upon being told she was not the star of the film

92

Opposite page: Lorelei and Dorothy in their dressing room. Russell was kind and supportive to Monroe throughout the filming of *Gentlemen Prefer Blondes*. Top: Monroe in her most famous musical number: "Diamonds Are a Girl's Best Friend." Bottom: In her 1985 "Material Girl" music video, Madonna famously paid homage to Monroe's "Diamonds Are a Girl's Best Friend" number.

How to Marry a Millionaire (1953)

Twentieth Century Fox

Director: Jean Negulesco

Screenplay: Nunnally Johnson

Based on plays by Zoe Akins, Dale Eunson and Katherine Albert

Principal Cast: Betty Grable (Loco Dempsey), Marilyn Monroe (Pola Debevoise), Lauren Bacall (Schatze Page), David Wayne (Freddie Denmark), Rory Calhoun (Eben), Cameron Mitchell (Tom Brookman), Alex D'Arcy (J. Stewart Merrill), Fred Clark (Waldo Brewster) and William Powell (J.D. Hanley)

In the 1950s, as cold war–era anxieties gripped the American public, the major motion picture studios faced a homegrown menace: the rising popularity of television. Desperate to lure audiences back into theaters, Twentieth Century Fox introduced CinemaScope, a technology that allowed for a wider image and better sound. The first film shot in CinemaScope, Jean Negulesco's *How to Marry a Millionaire*, had a second, even more potent weapon to combat the allure of television: the studio's newly anointed blonde box office bombshell, Marilyn Monroe.

Then riding sky-high on the success of *Gentlemen Prefer Blondes* (1953), Monroe was cast alongside one of Twentieth Century Fox's all-time biggest stars, Betty Grable, in this romantic comedy, based on Zoe Akins' play, *The Greeks Have a Word for It*. Although Grable had been one of the top-10 box office attractions for a decade, the popular star of such hit musicals as *The Dolly Sisters*

Top: Pola (Monroe), Loco (Betty Grable), and Schatze (Lauren Bacall) discuss the millionaires they want to find and marry. Middle: The roommates daydream about their night out on the town. Bottom: Schatze tries to reel in millionaire J.D. Hanley (William Powell) with her attentive gaze.

Pola (Marilyn Monroe) is pleased to learn that her millionaire date (Alex D'Arcy) is single.

(1945) and *Mother Wore Tights* (1947) was nearing the end of her reign as the queen of the Fox lot. When the casting of Monroe and Grable in *How to Marry a Millionaire* was announced, many observers believed that it marked the passing of the studio torch from Grable to her successor — and braced themselves for the inevitable catfight between the blonde bombshells. Grable, however, would have none of it. On the first day of filming, the actress warmly greeted Monroe in front of the crew and told her, "Honey, I've had it. Go get yours. It's your turn now."

For her part, Monroe refused to do anything, such as agree to pose in Grable's old dressing room, that would diminish her gracious co-star. Nevertheless, Twentieth Century Fox pushed Monroe to the forefront. In the film's opening credits Grable's name is listed first, but the film's advertising material switched the emphasis to Monroe, leaving little doubt as to which star was now the studio's favorite.

Adapted for the screen by Nunnally Johnson, *How to Marry a Millionaire* begins in an unconventional manner. To showcase the wide image and superior sound of CinemaScope, the film opens with a musical prologue, featuring conductor Alfred Newman leading an orchestra through a performance of his overture for *Street Scene* (1931); this sequence is followed by a montage of New York City scenes, accompanied

"Do you know who I'd like to marry?"

"Who?"

"Rockefeller."

"Which one?"

"I don't care."

– Pola (Monroe) telling her dream to Loco (Betty Grable)

by a jaunty musical score. This change in tempo paves the way for the introduction of the third member of the millionaire-seeking trio, the feisty model Schatze Page (Lauren Bacall).

Authoritative, cynical and still burned from her recent Reno divorce, Schatze is determined to snag a millionaire for her next husband. To increase her chances of meeting a rich spouse, she leases an apartment in a ritzy Manhattan neighborhood. There's just one problem: Schatze can't afford her plush new digs, so she takes on two other models as roommates, bubbly Loco Dempsey (Grable) and severely near-sighted Pola Debevoise (Monroe), who are also on the prowl for millionaires.

The trio takes advantage of chance encounters and makes the most of their opportunities to meet eligible men. However, as each woman pursues her quarry — in the nightclubs of New York, the slopes of Maine, and aboard a plane heading to Kansas City — she gradually realizes that the man who steals your heart isn't necessarily the one with the biggest bank account.

Monroe times four: Pola in the powder room. Opposite page: Pola (Monroe) models a fashionable swimsuit.

Admittedly, the characters Bacall, Grable and Monroe play are little more than stereotypes: the cynic, the party girl and the dumb blonde, respectively. Yet the stars manage to make these stock characters seem fresh, thanks to their genuine rapport and comedic flair. It's a revelation to see the film noir femme fatale Bacall toss off one-liners with deadpan aplomb. The ultra-glamorous Monroe generates some of the film's biggest laughs as her near-sighted character repeatedly stumbles and bumps into walls. And Grable is chipper and gung-ho throughout the film, especially when she gets to make an inside joke about her real-life marriage to big band leader Harry James.

Not to be outdone, Bacall and Monroe also get the chance to crack inside jokes. At one point, Bacall's Schatze expresses her preference for older men, like "that guy who was in *The African Queen*." Of course, "that guy" was Bacall's husband, Humphrey Bogart. And when Monroe's Pola is modeling a swimsuit studded with sparkly jewels, another character remarks that "diamonds are a girl's best friend" — a nod to Monroe's show-stopping musical number in *Gentlemen Prefer Blondes*.

"Is Mrs. Merrill here with you?"

"There is no Mrs. Merrill and I live in New York. Does that clear the situation a bit for you?"

"Oh yes, indeedy it does."

— Pola (Monroe) examining her date, Mr. Merrill (Alex D'Arcy)

Loco (Betty Grable) and Eben (Rory Calhoun) find love in the Maine snow.

In her 1978 memoir *Lauren Bacall By Myself*, Bacall noted that working with Monroe was often tedious. After sometimes waiting for hours for Monroe to appear on set, Bacall then had to endure Monroe checking with her acting coach, Natasha Lytess, for approval after each take. If Lytess disapproved, Monroe would ask to do it again. Bacall remembered, "A scene often went to fifteen or more takes…not easy, often irritating. And yet I didn't dislike Marilyn…. There was something sad about her — wanting to reach out — afraid to trust — uncomfortable. She made no effort for others and yet she was nice." Bacall had a much easier relationship with Betty Grable. According to screenwriter/producer Nunnally Johnson, Grable had a nickname for Miss Bacall: "Miss Bagel."

A resounding hit with audiences, *How to Marry a Millionaire* received generally favorable reviews, even as some critics quibbled about the film's well-worn premise.

"Men aren't attentive to girls who wear glasses."

— Pola (Monroe)

Top: The trio at their day jobs.
Bottom: Freddie Denmark
(David Wayne) notices
something odd about Pola's
reading habits.

But even these critics acknowledged that Monroe held a unique charm. In his *New York Times* review, Bosley Crowther wrote, "However, the baby-faced mugging of the famously shaped Miss Monroe does compensate in some measure for the truculence of Miss Bacall. Her natural reluctance to wear eyeglasses when she is spreading the glamour accounts for some funny farce business of missing signals and walking into walls."

While *How to Marry a Millionaire* may not rank among the screen's greatest comedies, this engaging and breezily funny film nevertheless ended Grable's Fox contract on a high note — and firmly established Monroe as an A-list star.

Schatze tells Tom Bookman (Cameron Mitchell) that she never wants to see him again.

"Honey, I've had it. Go get yours. It's your turn now."

— Betty Grable to Monroe on the first day of shooting

Top: I do? Schatze's wedding to J.D. Hanley. Bottom: The whole gang gathers at the local greasy spoon.

River of No Return (1954)

Twentieth Century Fox

Director: Otto Preminger

Screenplay: Frank Fenton

Principal Cast: Robert Mitchum (Matt Calder), Marilyn Monroe (Kay Weston), Rory Calhoun (Harry Weston) and Tommy Rettig (Mark Calder)

River of No Return began as a B-movie western, with a B-movie script penned by veteran Frank Fenton, whose previous credits included such forgettable horse operas as *Ride, Vaquero!* (1953) and *The Wild North* (1952). But Twentieth Century Fox was fighting to lure audiences away from their new TV sets with ultra-widescreen (2.55:1) CinemaScope, and studio chief Darryl F. Zanuck wanted to seal the deal with a star pairing. Robert Mitchum willingly climbed onboard, but Marilyn Monroe and Otto Preminger, both under contract, came to the project kicking and screaming.

Monroe didn't like her frontier dance-hall girl character, and Preminger felt the movie was beneath him. The notoriously controlling filmmaker was also furious that Monroe insisted her acting coach, Natasha Lytess, must "approve" every take. Before long, the star and her director weren't even talking to each other, and it fell to Mitchum to be the diplomatic go-between. But he agreed

Top: Frontier dance hall girl Kay Weston (Monroe) catches the eye of Matt Calder (Robert Mitchum). Bottom: Kay's fans: a rogue's gallery of unsavory characters.

with Preminger that Lytess' advice to enunciate every word was absolutely *wrong* for a period western. At one point Mitchum got so frustrated with Monroe's self-conscious line readings that he snapped at her, "Now stop that nonsense," slapped her backside, and said, "Let's play it like human beings. Come on!" After Lytess tried to coach child actor Tommy Rettig (of television's *Lassie*), Preminger banned her from the set. But he was ordered to reinstate her.

In the end, despite any on-set animosity and a stack of clichés as tall as the Canadian Rockies — which competed with the stars for the audience's attention — *River of No Return* turned out to be an above-average western and a respectable pairing of the rugged Mitchum and *Photoplay* magazine's most popular actress for 1954.

As Hedda Hopper's column reported, the stars' teaming marked "an interesting cycle, as Bob and Marilyn's ex-husband [Jim Dougherty] used to work together in an aircraft factory before either Mitchum or Monroe had ever turned to acting." The two had previously met casually, but this was the first time they had ever worked together. They got along fine, despite the hovering presence of Joe DiMaggio, who showed up on the sets at Banff and Jasper National Parks in Alberta, Canada, allegedly to "fish" but ostensibly to keep an eye on his wife and the handsome Mitchum. He couldn't have been too happy with a scene that has Mitchum giving her a rubdown, but there was no need

Top: Calder about to teach a trigger-happy cowboy some manners. Bottom: Calder shows his son Mark (Tommy Rettig) how to hold and shoot a rifle.

for jealousy. According to *Robert Mitchum: Baby, I Don't Care* by Lee Server, sources close to Mitchum reported that while the two got along fine, Monroe's leading man "never tried to bed her" because he saw in her "a frightened and possibly disturbed child-woman." Marilyn had an "unusually strong, debilitating menstruation" that sometimes got in the way of filming, but Mitchum was sympathetic. For her part, Monroe told an interviewer that "Mitch is one of the most interesting, fascinating men I have ever known."

Monroe's instincts were absolutely right, however, about her frontier dance-hall character. As a reviewer for the *Chicago Daily Tribune* observed, she "just doesn't seem comfortable as an outdoor type." Or maybe it's her glamorous image, dropped like a suitcase in the wilderness, that seemed so incongruous. But Preminger was equally out of his element. The Austrian director and writer Fenton give us a cast of characters so tame that you'd swear a teeth-grinding DiMaggio was standing in the wings on every saloon shot. While the beautiful Monroe struts her stuff as a skimpily costumed dance-hall singer, the supposedly rough-and-tumble miners who'll brawl and

Top: Kay and her gambler husband Harry (Rory Calhoun) brave the rapids. Monroe injured her leg while shooting on location. Opposite page: Matt and Mark can't resist stealing a peek at their beautiful guest.

shoot holes in the buckets of an errand boy are as well behaved as gentlemen at the opera. Not a one gets out of line. There's no leering or lusty remarks — only yearning looks when Monroe sings two dance-hall numbers, "I'm Gonna File My Claim" and "One Silver Dollar." She also does a nice job singing a version of the title song and a folksy little ditty ("Down in the Meadow") for Rettig, playing Mitchum's son.

"It is a toss-up whether the scenery or the adornment of Marilyn Monroe is the feature of greater attraction," a reviewer for the *Chicago Daily Tribune* observed. "The mountainous scenery is spectacular, but so, in her own way, is Miss Monroe." We have time to notice, though, because this river of a picture doesn't have much depth. The dialogue is mostly exposition or "hit-you-over-the-head" character reveals, and the plot is equally thin. We're introduced to Matt Calder (Mitchum) in an opening sequence that has him roaming a gold-rush camp looking for the son he hired someone to bring him after the boy's mother passed away. At the camp, young Mark (Rettig) had found a friend in the saloon singer Kay (Monroe), whose gambler husband Harry Weston (Rory Calhoun) wins a rich claim in a card game, but has to get to Council Bluffs to file before the miner can figure out he's been had.

"[*River of No Return*] was going to be a small thing, about 25 people, cast and crew sleeping in tents and eating at the campfire. All of a sudden [Darryl F.] Zanuck decided it was going to be a big picture with Marilyn and Mitchum, and Otto Preminger."

— Assistant director Paul Helmick

Later, the steady, sturdy Matt, whom we learn went to prison for killing a man to save a friend, is at his farm on the banks of the roaring river when he and Mark see a raft in trouble and haul it ashore. Aboard are Kay and Harry, who fights Calder and "borrows" his horse and rifle to go file that claim, leaving them defenseless against the local Native Americans. With no other choice, the unlikely trio tackles the most dangerous stretch of river to reach Council Bluffs and have that inevitable showdown with Weston.

At the time, reviewers were awestruck by the rapids scenes, but by today's movie standards it's painfully obvious that they were shot in the studio on a hydraulic platform in front of a giant process screen, while men reportedly stood at the sides and splashed the actors with buckets of water and shot "steel-headed arrows into the solid oak logs at their feet." The river was too dangerous for the stars to do their own stunts, so they were only on the raft while it was tethered to shore. Even then, Monroe badly injured her leg walking in the river and ended up in a cast.

Monroe and child actor Tommy Rettig, who starred in the television series *Lassie*.

"Next time you try a thing like that, I'll forget you're a woman."

"I doubt that."

— Matt Calder (Robert Mitchum) Weston (Monroe)

Top: Matt rubs Kay to get
the circulation back . . . and
titillate the audience. Bottom:
Roping dinner.

The stars' long-awaited
romantic clinch in *River of No
Return*. Bottom: Stunt doubles
were used in this exciting
sequence.

If the film bogs down, it's during the quiet scenes that are intended to establish a growing relationship between Matt and Kay. Those ring a little hollow, given that she married Weston because he was the only man who treated her like a lady, while Matt calls her a "tramp" with the same fierce judgment he pronounces on the Native Americans.

Narrative lapses aside, *River of No Return* is visually breathtaking, thanks to Joseph LaShelle's marvelous cinematography. Yet even the stunning vistas of the Canadian Rockies pale in comparison to the luminous spectacle of Monroe, sharing the screen with the ruggedly handsome Mitchum in their one and only film together.

"I think I deserve a better deal than a grade Z cowboy movie in which the acting finished second to the scenery and the CinemaScope process."

— Monroe

THERE'S NO BUSINESS LIKE SHOW BUSINESS (1954)

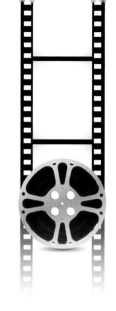

TWENTIETH CENTURY FOX

DIRECTOR: WALTER LANG

SCREENPLAY: PHOEBE AND HENRY EPHRON

PRINCIPAL CAST: ETHEL MERMAN (MOLLY DONAHUE), DONALD O'CONNOR (TIM DONAHUE), MARILYN MONROE (VICKY PARKER), DAN DAILEY (TERENCE DONAHUE), JOHNNIE RAY (STEVE DONAHUE) AND MITZI GAYNOR (KATY DONAHUE)

By 1954, Twentieth Century Fox had good reason to believe that audiences would rush to see *any* film starring Marilyn Monroe, then the biggest female film star in the world. Though she had earned her stardom with a variety of acting roles, ranging from light comedy to heavy drama, the studio executives decreed that Monroe's sex appeal would make the upcoming musical, *There's No Business Like Show Business*, an over-the-top sensation. So the film's husband-and-wife screenwriting team Henry and Phoebe Ephron (parents of writer/director Nora Ephron) created a role for Monroe; the studio reassigned songs to her; and veteran director Walter Lang (*Cheaper by the Dozen*) took the helm of the splashy musical. Taking on a part she did not choose was one obstacle for Monroe, but the prospect of sharing the screen with some of the biggest musical stars of the era was even more daunting.

There's No Business Like Show Business is a CinemaScope spectacle built around an almost breathless string of

Top: All in the family: Molly and Terence Donahue (Ethel Merman and Dan Dailey) bring their children into the act. Bottom: Showbiz gypsies: the Donahues take their act on the road.

Irving Berlin's most popular songs. The story centers on a family act, The Donahues, ready at any moment to burst into song, whose children join the act after happily training in vaudeville basics. Making up the family is a dream cast of singer-dancer-actors led by Broadway icon Ethel Merman as the brassy matriarch Molly and Dan Dailey — Betty Grable's frequent co-star in Fox musicals — as the kindly father Terence. Pop singer-turned-actor Johnnie Ray, firecracker Mitzi Gaynor and the amazing Donald O'Connor play their children Steve, Katy and Tim, respectively. Monroe co-stars as Vicky Parker, a sweet-natured hat check girl with her own dreams of stardom, whose life becomes entangled with the Donahue clan when Tim falls for her. Between musical numbers, Vicky and the Donahues experience show business successes large and small, with every one of them anxious to show what he or she can do on stage. In fact, *There's No Business Like Show Business* includes more singing than dialogue, as the actors croon, growl or belt Berlin's standards on enormous stage sets with legions of dancers — as well as in the Donahues' living room or on the street. Highlights include Monroe's stunning version of "After You Get What You Want," Ray doing "If You Believe," and Merman belting the show-stopping title song, which came to be her signature tune.

The care with which Monroe is placed in the film is difficult to ignore. Wearing extravagant, form-fitting costumes, she frequently appears against backdrops that literally sparkle. Her first appearance in the film is

Top: Hat check girl and aspiring singer Vicky Parker (Monroe) bewitches Tim Donahue (Donald O'Connor). Bottom: Vicky wows the audience with her nightclub act.

particularly strategic: after a full half-hour of vaudeville song and dance numbers, delivered by the wholesome Donahue clan, the audience gets its first glimpse of the glamorous Monroe, but only from behind. When she finally spins around to deliver her first line, it's clear the film has taken a turn as well.

The caliber of her co-stars was of little concern to Monroe at this difficult stage in her life. With a keen understanding of her box office appeal, and the money she was making for the studio, she felt she should have more creative control over her career, and resented the fact that her Fox contract required her to take whatever roles they assigned to her. As a compromise, Fox agreed to give Monroe the lead in Billy Wilder's *The Seven Year Itch* (1955) *if* she appeared in a supporting role in *There's No Business Like Show Business*, but she was unhappy with the arrangement, and more concessions were negotiated before production could begin. Most notably, Monroe wanted Fox to pay for her personal drama coach, Natasha Lytess, and her choice of music coach and dance director. Under pressure to hold on to the screen sensation, the studio begrudgingly agreed to Monroe's demands. Exacerbating tensions with the studio was the fact that Monroe was sick with bronchitis during part of the

At his farewell party before joining the priesthood, Steve Donahue (Johnnie Ray) delivers a rousing gospel tune.

"I much prefer working as a single, if you know what I mean. And I think you do."

— Vicky Parker (Monroe) to Tim Donahue (Donald O'Connor)

filming, and often showed up for work late, sleepy and unprepared.

Monroe's personal life while filming *There's No Business Like Show Business* added to the strain. Her marriage to retired baseball great Joe DiMaggio was starting to unravel, in part because of DiMaggio's unbending ideas about a proper wife's domestic role, and his jealousy over the time she spent with her coaches and on the set. Wary of the public-image machine so essential to the Hollywood system, he was annoyed at the attention Monroe received in the press, and furious at the overtly sexual nature of her dance scenes in the film; his reaction made it almost impossible for her to perform when he appeared on the set. Adding to their marital tensions were rumors that Monroe's relationship with her music director, Hal Schaefer, had become romantic. Just weeks after she finished shooting *There's No Business Like Show Business* Monroe filed for divorce from the Yankee slugger.

Monroe's feeling that the part of Vicky Parker was not a good career move was echoed by critics who loved the film, but questioned her part in the extravaganza. Television host Ed Sullivan pronounced her steamy rendition of "Heat Wave" "one of the most flagrant violations of good taste" he'd ever seen. His moralistic tone was echoed by the *New York Times'* Bosley Crowther, who sniped that Monroe's "wriggling and squirming to 'Heat Wave' and 'Lazy' are embarrassing to behold," though he also praised the film as "a major success." On a less prudish note, Crowther called the entire film — including Monroe's contribution — "one long gorgeous wallow in fantastical style and sentiment."

Top: Tim bumps into the girl of his dreams in a Miami nightclub. Bottom: Monroe sings "Heat Wave," a number originally intended for her co-star Ethel Merman.

"You can whistle 'Mandy,' do an 'Off to Buffalo,' and count the house at the same time — and tell me within five cents how much is out there."

— Terence Donahue (Dan Dailey) to Molly Donahue (Ethel Merman)

Opposite page: "The Five Donahues" reunite on stage to perform with Vicky. Top: Tim has marriage on his mind as he strolls with Vicky in the Miami moonlight. Bottom: Tim and sister Katy Donahue (Mitzi Gaynor) join Vicky to perform "Lazy."

The production values in *There's No Business Like Show Business* were the best the industry had to offer, and earned the film Academy Award nominations for costume design and musical score. But for all the glitzy spectacle, Monroe's earthy appeal and her sense of humor come through on-screen. The hard work she put into every part of her performance pays off and, like the best screen actors at the top of their game, the effort is invisible on the screen. Monroe seems to blend in happily with the great hoofers and song stylists, as if there's no place else she'd rather be than in *There's No Business Like Show Business*.

"It's different with me. I've been on my own since I was 15. This show is my big chance. It's make or break."

— Vicky Parker (Monroe) to Tim Donahue (Donald O'Connor)

THE SEVEN YEAR ITCH (1955)

TWENTIETH CENTURY FOX

DIRECTOR: BILLY WILDER

SCREENPLAY: BILLY WILDER AND GEORGE AXELROD

BASED ON THE PLAY BY AXELROD

PRINCIPAL CAST: TOM EWELL (RICHARD SHERMAN), MARILYN MONROE (THE GIRL), EVELYN KEYES (HELEN SHERMAN), ROBERT STRAUSS (KRUHULIK), OSCAR HOMOLKA (DR. LUDWIG BRUBAKER) AND SONNY TUFTS (TOM MACKENZIE)

Reveling in the skirt-billowing breeze from a subway grate, a sexually flamboyant Marilyn Monroe creates one of cinema's most iconic images in *The Seven Year Itch*. Her enthusiastic exhibitionism also raised temperatures in other ways. The late-night filming of the suggestive sequence in Manhattan, with a raucous crowd of onlookers, marked a climactic event in her short-lived marriage to Yankee outfielder Joe DiMaggio. A few months later, when a 52-foot-tall cutout of the shot was unveiled in front of the Loews State Theater in Times Square to promote the movie's opening, it was a media event and a pop-culture milestone. Although the scene in the finished film doesn't match the famous pose, it didn't affect Monroe's superstardom one little bit.

The affectionate, innuendo-laced comedy reflects a time when air conditioning was a rarity, and New York husbands with a little money sent their wives

Top: Richard Sherman (Tom Ewell) happily bids adieu to his wife (Evelyn Keyes) and annoying son for the summer. Bottom: Sherman's first sight of The Girl (Monroe) entering his apartment building.

and children out of town for a respite from the sweltering summers. Richard Sherman (Tom Ewell), a nondescript fellow on the cusp of 40, relishes the calm and quiet after his family is gone — until he meets the blonde bombshell (Monroe) who just moved into the building. Sherman's main asset is his imagination — he's the erstwhile creative director for a paperback publisher — and his mind goes into overdrive dreaming up seduction scenarios.

Monroe is perfectly cast as the naïve, nubile and not very bright object of Sherman's desire. The character isn't given a name and is merely identified in the credits as "The Girl," an acknowledgment that she isn't a three-dimensional person but a projection of Sherman's improbable fantasy: a promiscuous yet innocent ditz who's also capable of sophisticated sultriness when the occasion requires. The role closely corresponded to Monroe's screen persona, and also provided a pretty fair resemblance to the way moviegoers of both sexes perceived the real Marilyn.

But Monroe wasn't playing herself, and while everyone was gazing at a sex symbol, the comedienne turned in an effervescent, spot-on performance. "She was, believe it or not, an excellent dialogue actress," director Billy Wilder said. "She knew where the laugh was." That's no small achievement, especially since The Girl isn't provided with goals or needs, and exists solely as the trigger (Freudian pun intended) for Sherman's bumbling advances and neurotic self-incriminations.

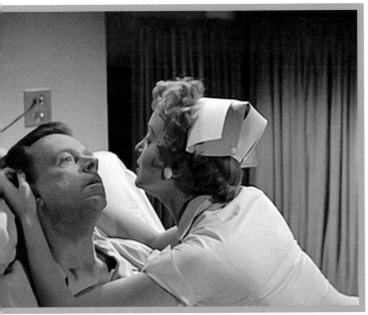

Top: Sherman ponders "The Repressed Urge in the Middle-Aged Male." Bottom: Sherman fantasizes about being ravished by a night nurse (Carolyn Jones).

Sherman seduces The Girl with Rachmaninoff — at least in his daydreams.

Sherman has been a model of fidelity for his seven years of marriage, notwithstanding "a kind of animal thing I've got," and the combination of lust, guilt, jealousy and panic adds up to a bona-fide midlife crisis. Of course, everyone from the producers to the ticket takers to the ticket buyers had the same thought: If you're going to be tempted, who better to be tempted by than Marilyn Monroe?

George Axelrod's hit play of the same name had run for three years on Broadway when Wilder, the brilliant and successful director of adult comedies, was hired to adapt it for the screen. However, the play's raciness had to be toned down to comply with the studio-adopted guidelines known as the Motion Picture Production Code, lest the censors object. Adultery could not be celebrated or condoned, which accounts for Sherman's excessive guilt feelings. Although he and The Girl consummate their affair in the play, that was verboten on-screen. Wilder tried to discreetly signal to the audience that the act had taken place with

"I think it's just elegant to have an imagination. I just have no imagination at all. I have lots of other things, but I have no imagination."

— The Girl (Monroe)

118

a shot of the maid finding a hatpin in Sherman's bed, but the censors wouldn't allow it. The net effect, unfortunately, is to make Sherman less worldly and more childish. Although *The Seven Year Itch* remains an altogether enjoyable and frequently delightful movie about the inflated male ego and puritanical American sexual mores, Wilder was frustrated that he couldn't make a more bitingly satirical picture.

Neither Ewell nor Vanessa Brown, the original stars of the Broadway production, was Wilder's first choice. The director tested and requested Walter Matthau, then a no-name actor with a batch of TV credits, but Twentieth Century Fox refused to accept an unknown. Monroe was in the picture all along (once she acceded to the studio's request that she play a supporting role in *There's No Business Like Show Business*), a smart choice regardless of how much trouble she was on the set. Chronically late and typically requiring dozens of takes to complete a scene, she drove the budget higher and higher. But the picture was a hit, as expected, and turned a sizable profit.

The Girl (Monroe) acts out her television pitch for toothpaste for Sherman's benefit.

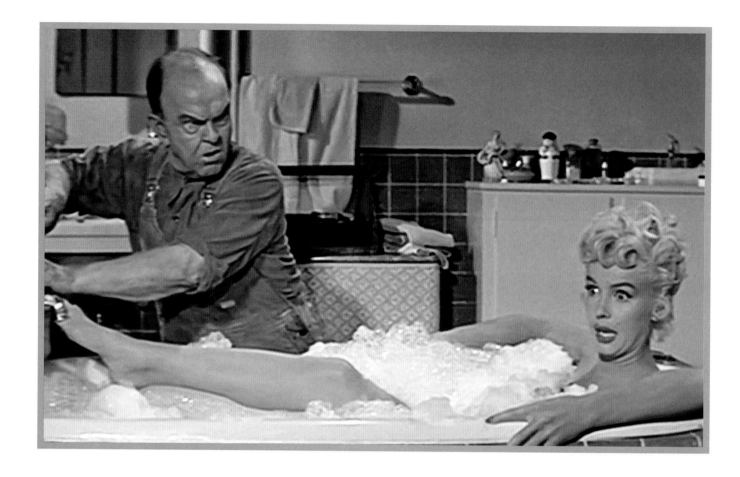

"It's very difficult to talk seriously about Monroe, because she was so glitzy, you know," Wilder recalled decades later. "She escaped the seriousness somehow; she changed the subject. Except she was very tough to work with. But what you had, by hook or crook, once you saw it on the screen, it was just amazing. Amazing, the radiation that came out."

The chief reasons for the picture's success, plainly, were Monroe's allure and the fine art of studio publicity. When she'd arrived in New York to shoot the picture, the first day was devoted to press interviews. Over the next week, the star and the production received saturation coverage in the media. Consequently, a reported crowd of 5,000 showed up at Lexington Avenue at 52nd Street shortly after midnight on Sept. 15, 1954, to watch Monroe shoot take after take of the skirt-blowing scene and snap pictures of her in between. "She loved the crowds," Wilder said. "She lifted a finger to her lips, they all quieted down, and we filmed some more."

The Girl patiently waits for the plumber (Victor Moore) to extricate her toe from the faucet. Opposite page top: Sherman imagines The Girl going on television to describe his lame seduction attempt. Bottom: The iconic shot of Monroe over the subway grate.

It Tickles ... It Tantalizes
... It's Terrific!

— *The Seven Year Itch* theatrical trailer

The only spectator not enjoying the late-night shoot was Joe DiMaggio, who left the scene in a fury. A screaming match ensued when Monroe returned to the hotel, and she showed up the next day with bruises on her shoulders. Two weeks later, she filed for divorce. The strains in their marriage were apparent long before that night in Manhattan, and stemmed in some measure from DiMaggio's distaste for Hollywood. The skirt-blowing scene was subsequently reshot on the Fox lot, which accounts for the discrepancy between the larger-than-life still photo of Monroe that graced the cutout and the panning shot from the waist down in the film.

On her 29th birthday, June 1, 1955, Marilyn Monroe was accompanied to the New York premiere of *The Seven Year Itch* by her plainly uncomfortable ex-husband Joe DiMaggio.

Sherman can't believe his ears when The Girl expresses her relief that he's married and "safer." Opposite page top: The Girl and Sherman enjoy a spirited duet — on "Chopsticks." Bottom: Sherman and The Girl have an unexpected guest.

"She thought the way she looked entitled her to special privileges. It was true. But it didn't work with me, because I looked at her not as a man, but as a director. Well, most of the time."

— Billy Wilder

BUS STOP (1956)

TWENTIETH CENTURY FOX

DIRECTOR: JOSHUA LOGAN

SCREENPLAY: GEORGE AXELROD

BASED ON THE PLAY BY WILLIAM INGE

PRINCIPAL CAST: MARILYN MONROE (CHERIE), DON MURRAY (BEAUREGARD "BO" DECKER), ARTHUR O'CONNELL (VIRGIL BLESSING), BETTY FIELD (GRACE), EILEEN HECKART (VERA), ROBERT BRAY (CARL) AND HOPE LANGE (ELMA DUCKWORTH)

Bus Stop came out more than a year after Monroe's previous hit movie, *The Seven Year Itch*. The period between those two movies was a tumultuous time for Monroe. Having divorced Joe DiMaggio, Monroe moved to New York for a year to study at Lee Strasberg's Actors' Studio. There, she strived to learn the realistic style of acting known as The Method. It was also during this time that she began a romance with the legendary playwright, Arthur Miller, whom she would later marry at the completion of *Bus Stop*.

Monroe's year in New York also marked a period of legal squabbles with Twentieth Century Fox. After much wrangling, Monroe returned to Los Angeles with her acting coach, Paula Strasberg (wife of Lee, mother of Susan) and her newfound clout to have director's approval on *Bus Stop*. Fox chose Joshua Logan, a Broadway director (*South Pacific*) turned film director, to helm the

Top: Virgil (Arthur O'Connell) finds Bo (Don Murray) "overdoing everything" again as Bo takes a shower and bath at the same time. Bottom: Cherie (Monroe) shows her friend Vera (Eileen Heckart) where she's been and where she hopes to go.

film adaptation of William Inge's play, *Bus Stop*. Monroe approved this decision. Joshua Logan later admitted that his first thoughts on Marilyn Monroe playing the part Kim Stanley originated on stage were not favorable. "Oh, no — Marilyn Monroe can't bring off *Bus Stop*. She can't act." Later, he recanted. "I could gargle with salt and vinegar even now as I say that, because I found her to be one of the greatest talents of all time."

Bus Stop opens on the Montana ranch of one Beauregard "Bo" Decker (Don Murray) as he practices his steer roping one last time before he heads out to a rodeo in Phoenix. A troublesome mix of brashness and naivety, Bo tells his pal and father figure, Virgil (Arthur O'Connell), that he's going to win every prize. Arthur tells the cocksure 21-year-old that it's time to think of other things than cows and horses. It's time to meet a woman. Bo warms to the idea and declares on the bus ride down to Phoenix that he's going to find his "angel."

Having never been off the ranch before, except for getting his tonsils out, Bo is an utter greenhorn in the ways of civilized life. At night, Virgil and Bo go to a local Phoenix saloon and there Bo meets his "angel." On stage, in fishnets and a body-hugging green costume, is Cherie (Marilyn Monroe), a down-on-her-luck, not too terribly talented, ex-Ozarks hillbilly turned chanteuse. She longs to go to Hollywood to be discovered and get some respect, but her financial picture dictates that she stay where she is. One look at Cherie and Bo is hooked. He jumps on a table and tells the rowdy group

Top: Cherie warbles "That Old Black Magic" to a saloon full of rowdy cowboys. Bottom: Bo (Don Murray) tears into the crowd for talking over Cherie's song.

Touched by an "angel": Bo falls head-over-heels in love with Cherie.

of cowboys to be quiet so that Cherie can sing her song. Cherie is grateful for the chivalry and meets with Bo after the show to share a kiss. When she tells him her name is Cherie, Bo decides that's too fancy and renames her, "Cherry." She protests this, but becomes truly unnerved when Bo announces that she is his "angel" and that he intends to marry her the next day. Virgil tells Bo that he can't command a woman to marry him, but Bo won't hear it.

The following day Bo wakes Cherie up, drags her to the rodeo, and stops her every attempt to elude him. By nightfall, Cherie finds herself kidnapped on a bus heading to Montana with Virgil and Bo. When the bus becomes trapped at a bus stop due to heavy snow, the other passengers become aware of Cherie's situation and Bo must face the reality of what he has done.

The tone of *Bus Stop* is an uneven blend of comedy, romance and melodrama. There are several laughs in the beginning, but the comedy lessens as Bo's campaign to win Cherie intensifies. His outrageous tactics never stray to outright violence against Cherie, but the lingering fear that they might is unsettling. Murray manages

"I ain't sung hillbilly since I was, well, not since I turned chanteuse."

— Cherie (Monroe)

126

to perform the unusual trick of coming across both as an aggressive, emotional steamroller while at the same time remaining an immature naif who actually harbors little malice.

Monroe attacks her role in true Method style. She speaks in an Ozarks accent while wearing the cheap clothes and unflattering makeup of a saloon floozie. This was conscious choice on her part. Before filming began, she rejected the costume designs offered her and searched the costume department for the more tawdry clothes she felt her character would wear.

To modern eyes, Monroe's acting may seem a touch overwrought. A frequent action of hers is to cover her face with her hands when things become too much. That said, it does appear that she was trying to reach a deeper level of craft and shake off the perception that she was just eye candy. Indeed, her purposely stumbling and off-key performance of "That Old Black Magic" comes as a striking contrast to the slick, glamorous performance of the "Diamonds Are A Girl's Best Friend" musical number in *Gentlemen Prefer Blondes* (1953).

When *Bus Stop* was released, Monroe was hailed in some quarters for her Method-inspired acting. In his *New York Times* review, Bosley Crowther raved, "Hold onto your chairs, everybody, and get set for a rattling surprise. Marilyn Monroe has finally proved herself an actress in *Bus Stop*. She and the picture are swell!" The film industry trade magazine *Variety* was not as enthusiastic. "Monroe comes off acceptably, even though failing to maintain any kind of consistency in the Southern accent."

Other critics weighed in as well. The Hollywood Foreign Press nominated Monroe as Best

Top: Cherie gives it her all for Bo's benefit. Bottom: Bo formally introduces himself to the object of his affection.

Cherie can't escape the attentions of her number one fan.

Actress-Drama and *Bus Stop* as Best Motion Picture-Drama, but neither the film nor Monroe won the Golden Globe. In the 1956 Oscar race, *Bus Stop* earned only one nomination, and it wasn't for Monroe. Don Murray was nominated as Best Supporting Actor, but did not win. Many viewed the lack of an Oscar nomination for Monroe as a snub from the film industry for her legal troubles with Twentieth Century Fox. Both the New York Times Critics and the National Board of Review named *Bus Stop* as one of the year's 10 best films. The public also had their say. *Bus Stop* came in as one of the top 20 box office successes of 1956.

"Now I come down for the rodeo tomorrow with the idea in mind of finding me an angel. And you're it."

— Bo (Don Murray)

Top: Cherie lashes out at Bo after he rips off the tail of her costume. Middle: Cherie sits trapped on a Montana-bound bus with Bo and Virgil. Bottom: Virgil and the bus driver (Robert Bray) try to stop Bo from carrying off Cherie.

THE PRINCE AND THE SHOWGIRL (1957)

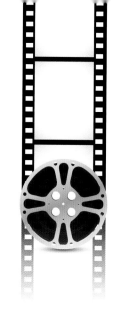

WARNER BROS. PICTURES

DIRECTOR: LAURENCE OLIVIER

SCREENPLAY: TERENCE RATTIGAN

BASED ON THE PLAY "THE SLEEPING PRINCE" BY RATTIGAN

PRINCIPAL CAST: MARILYN MONROE (ELSIE MARINA), LAURENCE OLIVIER (CHARLES, THE REGENT), SYBIL THORNDIKE (THE QUEEN DOWAGER) RICHARD WATTIS (NORTHBROOK) AND JEREMY SPENSER (KING NICOLAS)

What do you get when you take arguably the greatest actor of the twentieth century and team him with a Hollywood screen goddess? That's the intriguing question answered by *The Prince and the Showgirl*. By 1957, Laurence Olivier had solidified his reputation as a brilliant, classically trained actor and director of both stage and screen. Into his rarefied sphere came Marilyn Monroe, a glamorous star who embraced a diametrically opposed style of acting, the Method. Given the stars' profound personal and professional differences, there was bound to be some tension. Yet no one anticipated how quickly Olivier and Monroe's much ballyhooed teaming would degenerate into outright hostility, turning the filming of *The Prince and the Showgirl* into an endurance test for cast and crew.

Based on Terence Rattigan's play, *The Sleeping Prince, The Prince and the Showgirl* begins in England on the eve of the

Top: Elsie Marina (Monroe) performing onstage. Bottom: Grand Duke Charles, the prince regent (Laurence Olivier) meets the gorgeous showgirl backstage.

1911 coronation of King George V. The British Foreign Office is anxious to keep visiting dignitaries happy, so they send out one of their own, Peter Northbrook (Richard Wattis), to the Carpathian embassy. Upon arrival, Northbrook places himself at the service of the widowed Grand Duke Charles (Olivier), Regent of the Balkan state of Carpathia, his mother-in-law, the Queen Dowager (Sybil Thorndike) and his 16-year-old son, the future king (Jeremy Spenser).

Anxious to keep Charles entertained, Northbrook takes him to a theater revue, where Charles is immediately smitten with the gorgeous showgirl, Elsie Marina (Monroe). Through Northbrook, Charles invites Elsie to a midnight supper at the embassy, where he inexplicably ignores her to conduct official business. Irritated by his cavalier treatment, she pours herself several vodkas, to the point that she tipsily rebuffs Charles' awkward attempts to seduce her and collapses in a drunken stupor. Seething, he orders his men to take her away to sleep it off.

The next morning, Northbrook attempts to escort Elsie out of the embassy before the Queen Dowager sees her, but Charles' mother-in-law immediately spots the showgirl. A bit "vague" in the head, the Queen Dowager asks Elsie to join the Carpathian entourage to the coronation. Still in her white evening dress, Elsie complies — much to the shock of Charles, who eventually succumbs to Elsie's charms when they dance together at the coronation ball.

Top: Northbrook (Richard Wattis) pleads with Elsie to have dinner with Charles. Bottom: Charles pours the first of many drinks for Elsie.

Charles tries to seduce Elsie.

In February of 1956, Marilyn Monroe and Laurence Oliver held a joint press conference in New York to announce *The Prince and the Showgirl,* the first film to be produced by Marilyn Monroe Productions. In a room packed with reporters, the strap broke on Monroe's dress. From that point, any talk about the film or Olivier was abandoned, as the reporters' focus shifted entirely to Monroe. Although she swore it was a wardrobe malfunction, Olivier thought it was a deliberate ploy to steal the limelight. They were off to a rocky start, months before production began in England's Pinewood Studios.

Well aware that Monroe had a reputation for being "difficult," Olivier asked her *Bus Stop* director Josh Logan for advice. Logan advised him that he needed to be a calming force with the ultrasensitive sex symbol. If Olivier lost his temper or took a domineering tone with Monroe, she would lose her always fragile self-confidence and be unable to work.

In July of 1956, Monroe and her new husband of two weeks, playwright Arthur Miller, arrived in London in July to start production on *The Prince and the Showgirl.*

"Better luck next time, only not with me of course."

— Elsie Marina (Monroe)

Monroe also brought her Method acting coach, Paula Strasberg, who had been at Monroe's side throughout the filming of *Bus Stop*. Almost immediately, Olivier took issue with Strasberg's constant presence on the set — especially when he felt Monroe ignored *his* direction to follow Strasberg's advice.

Nor did Olivier follow Logan's advice about handling Monroe. Frustrated by her reliance on Strasberg, he was often condescending and insulting to Monroe, who withdrew, just as Logan had predicted. She began showing up late to the set or not at all; turned to prescription drugs to combat performance anxiety; and gained and lost weight so dramatically that several copies had to be made of the white dress she wears throughout the majority of the film. To make matters worse, she suffered from chronic insomnia during the production. Despite all the problems, co-star Dame Sybil Thorndike, took a more charitable attitude to Monroe than Olivier. "We need her desperately," she said, "She's the only one of us who knows how to act in front of the camera."

Neither critics nor audiences cared for *The Prince and the Showgirl,* which underperformed at the box office. In his *New York Times* review, Bosley Crowther wrote, "Miss Monroe mainly has to giggle, wiggle, breathe deeply and flirt. She does not make the showgirl a person, simply another of her pretty oddities."

That said, there are still joys to be found in *The Prince and the Showgirl.* The supporting players, particularly Wattis and Thorndike, deliver their dry, tart lines in winning fashion. Olivier mostly delivers a broad comedic performance, but his subtle reactions to Monroe are more engaging.

Top: Elsie tells the young king (Jeremy Spenser) that she's overheard his traitorous plan. Bottom: As Northbrook looks on, the Queen Dowager (Sybil Thorndike) speaks in French to a bewildered Elsie.

Monroe makes the most of a near-slapstick scene where she darts anxiously in and out of servants preparing supper. She looks beautiful in many scenes and has a wonderfully spontaneous laugh when she zings a particularly cutting line to Olivier's character.

A critical and commercial disappointment in the United States, *The Prince and the Showgirl* received a warmer reception in Europe. It was nominated for five BAFTAs (British Academy of Film and Television Awards) including Best British Actor, Best Foreign Actress and Best British Film. Although Monroe lost the BAFTA prize, she won the Italian David di Donatello Award for Best Actress.

"You know what's going to happen? I'm going to fall in love with you 'cause I always, always do."

— Elsie Marina (Monroe)

Opposite page: Elsie's behavior during the Coronation parade horrifies Northbrook. Top: Charles allows a slip of a smile for Elsie. Bottom: Elsie is moved by the majestic coronation ceremony.

Battle-scarred from working with Monroe on *The Prince and the Showgirl*, Olivier would not direct another film for 13 years, an adaptation of Anton Chekhov's *The Three Sisters* (1970). But after Monroe's death in 1962, Olivier put aside his rancor to deliver a poignant tribute to his former co-star: "No one had such a look of unconscious wisdom, and her personality was strong on the screen — she was quite wonderful, the best of all."

Elsie chats with the king at the coronation ball. Opposite page: Elsie tries to convince Charles to make amends with his son.

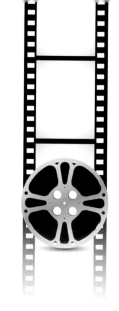

SOME LIKE IT HOT (1959)

UNITED ARTISTS

DIRECTOR: BILLY WILDER

SCREENPLAY: BILLY WILDER AND I.A.L. DIAMOND

PRINCIPAL CAST: MARILYN MONROE (SUGAR KANE
KOWALCYZK), TONY CURTIS (JOE), JACK LEMMON (JERRY),
GEORGE RAFT ("SPATS" COLUMBO), PAT O'BRIEN (MULLIGAN)
AND JOE E. BROWN (OSGOOD FIELDING III)

Sugar Kane, *Some Like It Hot*'s va-va-voom band singer who captures the rapt attention of cross-dressing Chicago musicians Joe (Tony Curtis) and Jerry (Jack Lemmon), fits Marilyn Monroe's voluptuous curves like a second skin. Yet filmgoers almost didn't get a chance to see the actress in the role that perfectly encapsulates her sexy comic genius. Director Billy Wilder intended the part for musical star Mitzi Gaynor, but Monroe read the script and exercised a star's prerogative, claiming the role for her own, and a classic comedy was born.

Forced to don drag as saxophonist Josephine (Curtis) and bassist Daphne (Lemmon) after witnessing the 1929 St. Valentine's Day Massacre, Joe and Jerry hide in plain sight as members of the all-girl orchestra, The Sweet Sues, where they encounter Sugar. Both guys are enchanted, but it is Joe who puts the moves on her once they've settled in for their gig at a grand Palm Beach hotel. Donning yet another persona, Joe sets about seducing Sugar in the guise of wealthy oil heir Junior (a wickedly funny send-up

Top: Joe (Tony Curtis) and Jerry (Jack Lemmon) play a "funeral" at Spats' speakeasy. Bottom: Joe and Jerry go on the lam as Josephine and Daphne.

of Cary Grant). Meanwhile, a real millionaire, Osgood Fielding III (Joe E. Brown), takes a fancy to Daphne, Jerry's drag alter ego, just as Chicago gangster "Spats" Columbo (George Raft) and his goons arrive, looking for Joe and Jerry.

Wilder and writing partner I.A.L. Diamond built a tightly constructed screenplay loosely inspired by a 1951 German film *Fanfaren der Liebe* (itself a remake of a 1935 French film *Fanfare d'amour*) that Wilder described as "deliriously bad." In contrast, every element of *Some Like It Hot* is precisely calibrated for maximum comic effect — even the maracas Jerry giddily shakes when he announces that clueless Osgood has proposed to Daphne. These maracas are no mere prop, but a way of separating the lines so that audience laughter would not swallow them. "I knew, when I cut back, I knew how long the laugh was gonna be," explained Wilder.

The laughs build continuously throughout the movie to end on one of the greatest punch lines in cinema history. Monroe might have recognized the script's genius when she read it, but David O. Selznick was shocked by the mayhem and black humor. After reading the script, the legendary producer blurted to Wilder, "Oh my God, you're not doing a comedy with *murder*. They're going to crucify you. They're going to walk on in *droves*! It's just going to be *embarrassing*!"

Wilder disagreed, recalling, "We were pretty sure it would be a good comedy. What we did not know was that it would be a great comedy."

Top: Sugar Kane (Monroe) takes center stage when The Sweet Sues rehearse. Bottom: Daphne and Sugar have a slumber party on the train.

Curtis was the first actor signed and Wilder intended to cast Frank Sinatra as Jerry along with Gaynor as Sugar. The director soon had second thoughts about Sinatra, telling Curtis, "He's going to be too much trouble. He'll have to dress up as a woman every day and I just can't see Frank doing that."

Gaynor had a lock on the female lead, especially since Wilder had vowed to never work with Monroe again after wrestling with her difficult personality during production of *The Seven Year Itch* (1955). Yet when she expressed interest in the part, Wilder's resolve went out the window: "It's wonderful that Monroe wanted to do the part. We had a big, big bomb there in that cannon that we could just shoot off. We would not have had that sex thing [without her]."

Wilder's fears about working with the mercurial star came true when Monroe wreaked havoc with her co-stars and the productions schedule, arriving late and sometimes not at all. A bigger issue was Monroe's memory. She might perform a three-minute scene letter-perfect, but then a simple line like, "Where's the bourbon?" might require over 50 takes. Wilder warned Curtis and Lemmon, "Whenever she

"I have this thing about saxophone players, especially tenor sax. They just curdle me. I don't know what it is, all they have to do is play eight bars of 'Come to Me, My Melancholy Baby,' and my spine turns to custard. I get goose pimply all over, and I come to 'em."

— Sugar Kane (Monroe)

gets it right, I'm going to print it, so keep your fingers out of places you don't want them to be."

Curtis later insisted that his famous insult, "Kissing Marilyn is like kissing Hitler," was meant as a joke, a stupid answer to a stupid question posed by a crew member, but he also compared working with her to serving in the Foreign Legion. Wilder could sympathize with his frustration: "We had many takes over the shoulders of the guys and they had to be standing on those high platform shoes. That hurts if you're not used to it."

The experience of making *Some Like It Hot* was not a completely painful one for Curtis. Soon after he came to Hollywood in the late 1940s, he and Monroe had a brief affair that left him with fond memories that he revisited as they shot their big love scene. "We did that scene over and over and I loved every take of it. We were revisiting the feelings we had for each other years earlier," he recalled. "I knew she was enjoying those memories as much as I was, although we never spoke of them."

Opposite page: Joe poses as millionaire oilman "Junior" to win Sugar's affections in Palm Beach. Bottom: Sugar's voluptuous shape and startling outfit wows the crowd as much as her singing.

When *Some Like It Hot* opened on February 5, 1959, *Variety* raved, "It's a wacky, clever, farcical comedy that starts off like a firecracker and keeps on throwing off lively sparks." Other reviews were mixed. Bosley Crowther in *The New York Times* declared the movie, "overlong, occasionally labored but often outrageously funny," while *Time* was downright churlish in pronouncing, "As for Marilyn, she's been trimmer, slimmer and sexier in earlier pictures."

The box office was more positive, as *Some Like It Hot* racked up $8.3 million in rentals for United Artists. Nominated for six Academy Awards, including Best Director, Best Screenplay (based on material from another medium) and Best Actor (Lemmon), it won one for Orry-Kelly's costumes. The Golden Globe awards were more generous, naming the film the Best Motion Picture-Musical or Comedy and Lemmon and Monroe the Best Actor and Actress prizes in the musical or comedy category. In 1989, the National Film Preservation Board

"She suggests sex. It *must* be better to be subdued, seduced and screwed by Marilyn Monroe — what could be better?"

— Billy Wilder, explaining why Sugar Kane (Monroe) is the aggressor in her love scene with Junior (Tony Curtis)

"She was naughty. She was like a mean seven-year-old girl. She would fall on me and grind me, not only with her mouth but in a few other places, and she would wait until I would get aroused then she'd get up off me."

—Tony Curtis on his love scenes with Monroe

Opposite page: Sugar steams up "Junior's" glasses. Top: "Why would a guy want to marry a guy?" "Security!" Bottom: Sugar pours her broken heart out to Daphne and Josephine while showing off her diamond bracelet consolation prize.

added the movie to the National Film Registry. In 1998, the American Film Institute named *Some Like It Hot* the number 14 movie of all time; in 2000, the AFI named Wilder's film the greatest comedy of all time. It's also the most beloved of Monroe's films and an ideal showcase for her inimitable combination of sensual abandon, innocence and perfect comic timing.

"I'm through with love." Sugar wails a torch song.

"Marilyn Monroe was magic. You couldn't take your eyes off her. Every guy wanted to take her home in his pocket. She was absolutely adorable, because she had that quality of sexiness mixed with innocence."

— *Some Like It Hot* cast member Sandra Warner

Top: Success! "Junior" succumbs to Sugar's charms. Below: Happily ever after? Millionaire Osgood Fielding III (Joe E. Brown) and Jerry.

PART 3

1960-1962

MARILYN MONROE: 1960-1962

Marilyn Monroe began the decade basking in the glow of her recent smash, *Some Like It Hot* (1959). In early 1960, she picked up a Golden Globe for Best Actress–Musical or Comedy and was planning to start her passion project, the Arthur Miller–penned. *The Misfits* (1961). However, the executives at Twentieth Century Fox had other ideas. Neither *Some Like It Hot* nor *The Misfits* were Fox properties, yet Monroe had a contractual obligation to the studio. Pinned down, Monroe agreed to make her next film a studio project: *Let's Make Love* (1960).

The film is probably best remembered for the high-profile love affair that developed between its two stars, Monroe and French actor Yves Montand. Lasting only for the duration of filming, Montand broke off the affair to return to his wife, Simone Signoret. Monroe returned to her husband, Arthur Miller, but their marriage was seriously damaged.

In July of 1960, with tensions high between them, Miller and Monroe reported to the Reno set of John Huston's *The Misfits*. What was supposed to be a dream project, with a cast comprised of Clark Gable, Montgomery Clift, Eli Wallach and Thelma Ritter, became a nightmare. Monroe delved heavily into prescription drugs and her resulting erratic behavior nearly derailed the film. Despite the many problems that plagued the set, *The Misfits* was completed in early November 1960.

> "He's a brilliant man and a wonderful writer, but I think he is a better writer than a husband."
>
> — Monroe on Arthur Miller

As it turned out, that month of November became a critical time in Monroe's life. Within two weeks of wrapping *The Misfits*, Monroe announced that her marriage with Miller was over and Clark Gable died after suffering a massive heart attack. Kay Gable, Gable's pregnant widow, publicly accused Monroe of contributing to his death by creating such a stressful environment on *The Misfits*. As Monroe had adored Gable since she was a child, this accusation sent her into a deep depression. Her psychiatrist at the time, Dr. Kris, became concerned and recommended that she commit herself to the Payne-Whitney Clinic. Monroe followed his recommendation and was horrified by what she considered the prisonlike conditions at Payne-Whitney. Desperate to get out, she contacted the man who she knew would help her, Joe DiMaggio.

DiMaggio arranged for Monroe to be transferred to Columbia-Presbyterian Medical Center, where she remained for three weeks. When she was released from the hospital, she was greeted by an unruly press mob that blocked her way to her car. Monroe spent the following months attending to various medical problems and did not shoot another film for the entirety of 1961.

That same year, Monroe watched Audrey Hepburn win accolades for her starring role in *Breakfast at Tiffany's* (1961). The author of the novella, Truman Capote, had wanted Monroe for the part of Holly Golightly, but it was not to be. Conflicting stories have Monroe turning down the part under Paula Strasberg's advice and producers rejecting Monroe because they felt Hepburn was the stronger actress. Other projects that Monroe seriously considered, but never came to fruition, were a biography of her idol, Jean Harlow, and a musical adaptation of *A Tree Grows in Brooklyn*.

After winning the Golden Globe in early 1962 as the World Film Favorite (Female), Monroe began shooting the Fox project *Something's Got to Give* in April of that year. Fox executives, who were already feeling the heat from the rampant cost overruns on another film, *Cleopatra* (1963), were alarmed by Monroe's chronic lateness and absenteeism. The situation escalated when Monroe appeared in Madison Square Garden to sing "Happy Birthday" to President Kennedy. Enraged that Monroe was somehow healthy enough to fly to New York, but not well enough to appear on a Los Angeles soundstage, the powers-that-be fired Monroe on June 8, 1962.

Less than two months later, amid rumors of affairs with both John F. Kennedy and his brother Robert, Marilyn Monroe died in her home on August 5, 1962. The cause of her death was an overdose of prescription pills. Whether it was an accident, a suicide, or as some conspiracy theorists insist, a murder, the fact remained that Monroe was gone. Once again, Joe DiMaggio stepped forward. Along with Monroe's half-sister and Monroe's secretary, DiMaggio arranged the funeral services. On August 8, 1962, amidst a small group of friends, Lee Strasberg delivered the eulogy and Marilyn Monroe was laid to rest.

> "I've never been in a Hollywood fight or feud. I have the most wonderful memory for forgetting things."
>
> — Monroe

MONROE'S LEADING MEN, 1960-1962

CLARK GABLE
The Misfits (1961)

The "King of Hollywood," Gable was a "man's man" whose 67 films include some of the greatest films of Hollywood's golden era; during his 1930s-era heyday, he starred in three Best Picture winners: *It Happened One Night* (1934), *Mutiny on the Bounty* (1935) and the film for which he is most remembered, *Gone with the Wind* (1939). Less than two weeks after filming wrapped on *The Misfits*, Gable died of a heart attack at the age of 59.

DEAN MARTIN
Something's Got to Give (1962)

A charter member of the "Rat Pack" and former straight man to Jerry Lewis, Martin may not have been a critic's darling, but he was a capable actor and fine light comedian. After testing his dramatic range in *Some Come Running* (1958) and *The Young Lions* (1958), Martin spent most of the 1960s starring in breezy comedies and the tongue-in-cheek Matt Helm spy films. He also headlined a popular television series, *The Dean Martin Show*,

YVES MONTAND
Let's Make Love (1960)

The Italian-born French film star made a handful of American films after *Let's Make Love* (1960), most notably *Grand Prix* (1966) opposite James Garner and *On a Clear Day You Can See Forever* (1970), starring Barbra Streisand. None of these films, however, did much to boost Montand's Hollywood profile. He found much more artistically and commercially rewarding roles in French cinema, where he starred in *The War Is Over* (1966), *Z* (1969) and *Jean de Florette* (1986).

LET'S MAKE LOVE (1960)

TWENTIETH CENTURY FOX

DIRECTOR: GEORGE CUKOR

SCREENPLAY: NORMAN KRASNA, HAL KANTER AND ARTHUR MILLER (UNCREDITED)

PRINCIPAL CAST: MARILYN MONROE (AMANDA DELL), YVES MONTAND (JEAN-MARC CLEMENT/ALEXANDER DUMAS), TONY RANDALL (ALEXANDER COFFMAN) AND FRANKIE VAUGHAN (TONY DANTON)

Marilyn Monroe's penultimate film *Let's Make Love* (1960) received a mixed reaction from audiences and critics alike. Some reviewers, like Bosley Crowther of the *New York Times*, pretty much dismissed it outright, calling it "a loggy affair."

Perhaps *Let's Make Love* suffered in comparison to Monroe's previous film, the universally acclaimed *Some Like It Hot* (1959). Whatever the reason, one thing is now certain: *Let's Make Love* is overdue for reevaluation. It is a thoroughly charming piece of glossy entertainment, featuring Monroe and French co-star Yves Montand at their most charismatic, and arguably one of Monroe's most underrated films.

A loose remake of the musical *On the Avenue* (1937) starring Dick Powell and Madeleine Carroll, *Let's Make Love* opens on billionaire Jean-Marc Clement (Montand,

Top: George Welch (Wilfred Hyde White) admonishes Jean-Marc Clement (Yves Montand) for all the attention created by his scandalous behavior. Bottom: Amanda Dell (Monroe) sings Cole Porter's "My Heart Belongs to Daddy," a song loaded with subtext and double entendres.

making his American film debut). A notorious womanizer, Clement is a tabloid fixture whose antics have inspired an off-Broadway theatrical company to satirize him in a musical revue. In an effort at damage control, Clement's public relations advisor Howard Coffman (the inimitable Tony Randall) urges him to attend one of the company's rehearsals.

What was meant to be nothing more than a photo op soon turns into something far more complicated when Clement sees singer/dancer Amanda Dell (Monroe) rehearsing her opening number. Then, in an "only in Hollywood" plot twist, the revue's director and cast members mistake Clement for an actor, auditioning to play the billionaire in the revue. Determined to turn his legendary charms on Amanda, Clement takes the role — going by "Alexandre Dumas" to protect his identity. Yet for all his *savoir faire*, Amanda remains cool to Clement's advances. As Clement struggles to woo the beautiful Amanda, he goes all out to prove himself an entertainer, hiring showbiz greats Milton Berle, Bing Crosby and Gene Kelly to tutor him, but the elaborate ruse nearly backfires on him.

Best known in the United States for such films as *The Wages of Fear* (1953) and *The Witches of Salem* (1958) and his one-man Broadway show, Montand was not the first actor offered the role of Clement. Gregory Peck was originally cast but left the film, complaining that the role of Clement had

Top: Monroe at her most alluring in *Let's Make Love*.
Bottom: Yves Montand, one of the greatest stars of French cinema.

been minimized — and that the script "was now about as funny as pushing Grandma down the stairs in the wheelchair."

After Peck's departure, Cary Grant, Charlton Heston, Rock Hudson, James Stewart and Yul Brynner reportedly turned down the role. As good as they would have been, there is something special in Montand's detached yet passionate approach to the role that is exactly right. The role of Clement also demands that Montand rise to the task of a sophisticate masquerading as an awkward, and a fine actor having to play a bad actor. Montand acquits himself with a bravura and convincing performance.

While Montand has the meatier role, Monroe's Amanda is the uncontested main attraction of *Let's Make Love*. Sliding down a pole in her opening number, Monroe makes one of the most eye-catching star entrances in musical film history. After breathily introducing herself with the line "My name is Lolita and I'm not allowed to play...with boys," she launches into Cole Porter's "My Heart Belongs to Daddy," an erotically charged production number laden

The ice begins to thaw between the French billionaire and the musical comedy star.

"Monroe, of course, is a sheer delight."

— *Variety* review, 1960

152

with subtext and double entendres. Although some reviewers complained that Monroe looks slightly overweight in *Let's Make Love*, she is nonetheless at her most voluptuously beautiful in her only *completed* film with legendary "woman's director" Cukor. Radiating her trademark blend of innocence, vulnerability and sensuality opposite Montand, Monroe truly does "light up like neon," as she sings in *Let's Make Love*. Their sizzling chemistry was fueled by a torrid affair off screen — they had adjoining bungalows at the Beverly Hills Hotel — that nearly destroyed Montand's long marriage to French film star Simone Signoret. The affair also marked the beginning of the end for Monroe and husband Arthur Miller, who did an uncredited polish on the screenplay.

The stars' headline-generating liaison overshadowed the film itself, which features Cukor's elegantly staged production numbers and songs by Cole Porter and the songwriting team of Sammy Cahn and James Van Heusen, who penned such Frank Sinatra standards as "High Hopes" and "Love and Marriage." Monroe and Montand also receive nimble comic support from Randall, the ever reliable character actor Wilfred Hyde-White (as Clement's

Montand and Monroe apparently took the film's title literally. Their steamy affair during the filming of *Let's Make Love* nearly ended Montand's marriage to Simone Signoret.

right-hand man) and British pop star Frankie Vaughan (playing Amanda's actor boyfriend). As for the celebrity cameos, Milton Berle is flat-out hilarious; he reportedly took out ads in Hollywood trade papers in a tongue-in-cheek bid for a Best Supporting Actor nomination.

Despite mixed notices, *Let's Make Love* received a Golden Globe nomination for Best Motion Picture (Musical) and a British Academy Award nomination for Best Film, as well as one for Best Foreign Actor (Yves Montand). The Writers Guild of America also nominated the film for Best Written American Musical (Norman Krasna and Hal Kanter), and the film received an Academy

"If she was a victim of any kind, she was a victim of her friends."

— *Let's Make Love* director George Cukor on Monroe

154

Opposite page: Dangerous
curves: Monroe's voluptuous
figure in *Let's Make Love*. Top:
Diamonds are a girl's best
friend: Amanda admires a gift
from Clement. Bottom: Tony
Randall (left, with actor Dennis
King Jr.) mines comic gold
as Clement's harried public
relations flack in *Let's Make
Love*.

Award nomination for Best Music Scoring (the work of the brilliant Lionel Newman).

Let's Make Love is a terrific rainy-day movie that's multilayered and richly textured. Granted, it's not a seamless piece of work, but *Let's Make Love* is nonetheless still worth seeing, if only for Monroe's performance, which director Cukor accurately called "quite dazzling."

One of the lavishly staged musical numbers in *Let's Make Love*. Opposite page top: Montand and Monroe duet. Bottom: Clement and Amanda go out on the town.

THE MISFITS (1961)

UNITED ARTISTS

DIRECTOR: JOHN HUSTON

SCREENWRITER: ARTHUR MILLER

PRINCIPAL CAST: MARILYN MONROE (ROSLYN TABER), CLARK GABLE (GAY FERLAND), MONTGOMERY CLIFT (PERCE HOWLAND), ELI WALLACH (GUIDO) AND THELMA RITTER (ISABELLE STEERS)

Written specifically for Marilyn Monroe, *The Misfits* was meant to be playwright Arthur Miller's gift to his troubled wife. As he envisioned it, the character of divorcee Roslyn Taber would prove, once and for all, that Hollywood's reigning sex goddess was also one of its most talented actresses. The part emphasizes the lush sexuality that made her a star, but also her vulnerability and sadness. Monroe delivers an emotional performance that is absolutely breathtaking in what would be her final completed film. Chaos and acrimony reigned behind the scenes, but John Huston's luminous black-and-white drama reflects only its forlorn characters' poignant circumstances.

"Cowboys are the last real men in the world, and they're about as reliable as jackrabbits," warns Roslyn's friend Isabelle Steers (Thelma Ritter) after they meet cowpoke Gay Ferland (Clark Gable) and his pilot pal Guido (Eli Wallach) in a Reno bar. At loose ends after her final decree, Roslyn falls in with the men, who are both

Top: Roslyn Taber (Marilyn Monroe) makes a memorable entrance. Bottom: Gay Ferland (Clark Gable) and Guido (Eli Wallach) survey the possibilities over drinks.

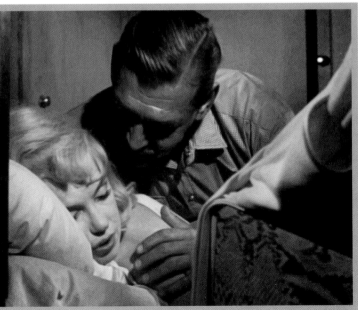

captivated by her beauty and her sensitivity. Gay draws her into his fiercely independent orbit while his passion for her awakens his long-dormant domestic side. A trip to the desert with Guido and rodeo rider Perce Howland (Montgomery Clift) to capture wild mustangs threatens the couple's fragile happiness, however, when Roslyn is horrified by their callous treatment of the horses.

An elegiac tone pervades the film that Miller described to Gable as "a sort of eastern western." These are cowboys that time has passed by, struggling to survive out in the great expanse of desert where the mustangs are fewer and fewer. The three men see a savior in Roslyn, but she is as adrift as they are, too aware of the way people inadvertently mistreat each other even when they're gripped by an existential crisis. "We're all dying, aren't we? We aren't teaching each other what we really know, are we?" she avers. All of them have been damaged by the impermanence of relationships, but that hasn't stopped their longing for connection.

Myths have grown up around the making of *The Misfits*, the biggest one that making it somehow killed its top-lined stars — starting with Gable, who died of a massive heart attack only days after the movie wrapped. The 59-year-old actor's insistence on performing rigorous stunts that included being dragged by a truck perhaps did contribute to his death, but 36-year-old Monroe's fatal 1962 overdose or the heart trouble that felled 46-year-old Clift in 1966 can hardly be blamed on any movie curse.

Top: Gay introduces himself to Roslyn. Bottom: Gay caresses a sleeping Roslyn.

Roslyn, Gay and Guido hit the road with Isabelle (Thelma Ritter).

What is true is that *The Misfits* was an extraordinarily difficult shoot, a far cry from Miller's original aim. While living in Reno awaiting his own final decree from his first marriage, Miller met a group of cowboys who inspired him to write "The Misfits," a short story that appeared in *Esquire* in 1957. Visiting Miller while Monroe was recovering from a miscarriage, photographer Stan Shaw told the playwright that his short story would make an ideal vehicle for Monroe: "[Roslyn's] a woman's part she could kick into the stands."

Shaw's idea galvanized Miller into writing a screenplay that would give his bride the serious, multilayered role she craved — like Betty Preisser, the female lead in the film version of Paddy Chayefsky's Broadway hit *Middle of the Night* (1959), which had gone instead to Kim Novak.

"I think you're the saddest girl I ever met."

— Gay Ferland (Clark Gable) to Roslyn Taber (Monroe)

160

Miller also wanted Huston to direct *The Misfits*. Although he had a reputation for running roughshod over actors, he had nevertheless been kind to Monroe early in her career, when they had worked together on *The Asphalt Jungle* (1950). The presence of Gable, Monroe's childhood idol, was another sweetener for the fragile star, who had once fantasized that the screen legend dubbed the "King of Hollywood" was her real father.

Monroe made two films while waiting to start *The Misfits*, *Some Like It Hot* (1959) and *Let's Make Love* (1960). Her affair with Yves Montand, her co-star in the latter, was still in bloom when shooting commenced on *The Misfits* in the summer of 1960. Miller's good intentions in writing a film for his wife had truly paved the way to a kind of hell, as the couple's marriage deteriorated rapidly during *The Misfits'* production.

"Something had happened in the relationship that was tearing it apart," observed Eli Wallach. "She was torn, conflicted either in one area with her real life and the acting life as this woman Roslyn. If you see the movie carefully, you'll see how vulnerable she was, how unhappy she was."

Monroe's pain manifested itself in a real way throughout the shoot. Her increasingly late arrivals on set left cast and crew waiting in temperatures that could soar to 110 degrees and created delays that sent the film over budget. Her barbiturate use was so acute that it threatened to derail the movie, until Huston arranged for her to detox for 10 days at a Los Angeles hospital. Monroe also had trouble with her lines; according to Miller, she kept insisting that it was the emotion, rather than the words, that was important. Playing the

Top: Gay's old friend Perce (Montgomery Clift) makes the acquaintance of Roslyn. Bottom: Roslyn comforts Perce as she listens to his life story.

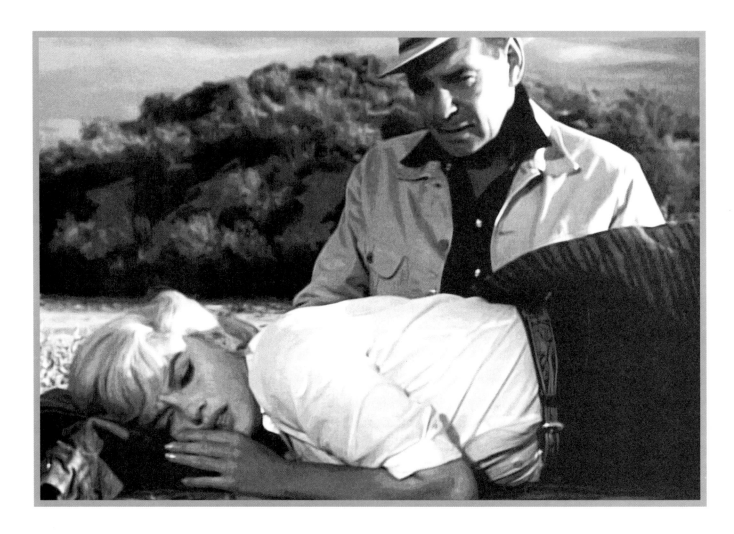

Guy attempts to soothe an upset Roslyn after she learns the truth about the mustangs.

small role of Roslyn's ex-husband, Kevin McCarthy recalled doing 17 takes with his back to the camera while Monroe struggled with her speech, until Huston finally gave up and moved on, depriving the actor of his reaction shots.

The Misfits opened in February 1, 1961, to critical disdain. Time magazine declared, "It is a dozen pictures rolled into one. Most of them, unfortunately, are terrible." Bosley Crowther in the New York Times found the characters amusing, but concluded, "They are shallow and inconsequential, and that is the dang-busted trouble with this film." Pauline Kael thought the movie was affecting but also erratic with "an uncomfortable element of fake psychodrama." The public was equally unimpressed with The Misfits. Costing $4 million to make, the most expensive black-and-white film ever made at that time, it earned only $4.1 million at the box office.

"Honey, when you smile, it's like the sun comin' up."

— Gay Ferland (Clark Gable) to Roslyn Taber (Monroe)

"I thought there was a greatness of spirit in her that the right role might release and that if that happened she might step out of herself and see her own worth."

—— Arthur Miller on wife Monroe in *The Misfits*

Top: Roslyn is appalled watching the men lasso wild horses. Bottom: Perce and Roslyn in a quiet moment.

"She's kind of hard to figure out. One minute she looks kind of dumb, brand new, like a kid. And then the next minute, she — but she moves, though, don't she?"

— Guido (Eli Wallach) to Gay Ferland (Clark Gable)

Top: Gay struggles to break the wild stallion. Bottom: Roslyn and Gay ride off into an uncertain future.

Despite the film's failure, the Directors Guild of America nominated Huston for his achievement and Monroe received the Henrietta Award at the 1962 Golden Globes for World Film Favorite (Female). The 1961 notorious bomb has proven in subsequent decades to be surprisingly resilient, continuing to attract new audiences, a testament to the film's evocation of a vanished way of life and Monroe's heartbreaking performance.

An exhausted Gay, broken by the stallion. Doing his own stunts may have contributed to Gable's fatal heart attack.

Something's Got to Give (1962)

Twentieth Century Fox
Director: George Cukor
Screenplay: Walter Bernstein and Nunnally Johnson
Principal Cast: Marilyn Monroe (Ellen), Dean Martin (Nick) and Cyd Charisse (Bianca)

In 1962, Twentieth Century Fox was hemorrhaging money, much of the bleeding stemming from the production of the Elizabeth Taylor-Richard Burton-starring epic *Cleopatra* (1963). With that never-ending shoot entering its fourth year, the studio badly needed a hit. Apparently unfazed by its dealings with the sickly, scandal-prone Taylor, Fox turned to the sickly, scandal-prone Marilyn Monroe to turn its fortunes around by casting her in *Something's Got to Give*, a remake of the classic screwball comedy *My Favorite Wife* (1940). *Something's Got to Give* turned out to be a prophetic title as Monroe's erratic behavior doomed the production. The studio fired her on June 8, 1962. Less than two months later, on August 5, her demons overtook her and she died of an overdose at age 36.

Included as part of Patty Ivins Specht's 2001 documentary *Marilyn Monroe: The Final Days*, a 37-minute edition of the film culled from 500 hours of footage

Top: A camera and makeup test shot for *Something's Got to Give*. Bottom: Monroe with her $5,000 per week acting teacher Paula Strasberg. It was Strasberg she turned to for approval after a take, not her director.

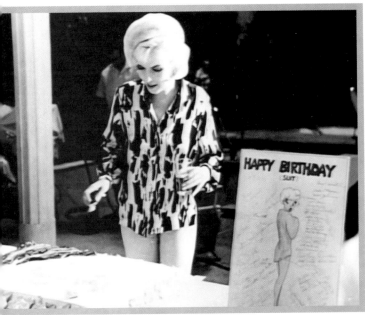

provides a tantalizing glimpse of what might have been. Monroe plays a woman long thought dead who reappears in husband Dean Martin's life just after he has acquired a second wife (Cyd Charisse). A frothy romantic comedy, it may well have become the big hit Fox so desperately wanted. The easy rapport between Monroe and Martin is delightful, and co-star Charisse is hilarious as the in-the-dark bride. As if that weren't enough, there is the scene that would have tested the Production Code's rigid boundaries while wowing Monroe's fans: a nude Monroe not only skinny dipping, but also showing off her famous body as she dries herself poolside.

What was missing at the start was a final script, an assignment that had defeated Fox staff writer Arnold Schulman. Nunnally Johnson, who had written Monroe's 1953 hit *How to Marry a Millionaire*, was brought in to write the screenplay. No one consulted director George Cukor. When he finally read Johnson's script, he thought it lacked the charm of Sam and Bella Spewack's Oscar-nominated *My Favorite Wife* screenplay. The director recruited formerly blacklisted screenwriter Walter Bernstein for another rewrite. Before Cukor ever shot a frame of film, *Something's Got to Give* was already $300,000 over budget.

Monroe and her *Let's Make Love* director's renewed relationship was already getting off to a shaky start when Cukor angered Monroe by failing to oversee her makeup and costume tests. But over the course of the production, it was Monroe's absences that would

Top: Wally Cox and Monroe prepare to shoot a scene on Monroe's birthday, June 1. Bottom: Monroe caps a rare full day of shooting by celebrating her birthday on set with cast and crew.

cause havoc. After spending a week in New York working with acting teacher Lee Strasberg on her part, she called in sick with the flu and sinusitis the very first day of shooting on April 23. She was absent the entire first week, forcing Cukor to reconfigure the production schedule, bringing in Charisse to shoot her scenes weeks before he thought he would need her.

Those first days set a pattern that would continue throughout the production. On May 7, Monroe called in sick for the tenth time. Not all of her absences were due to illness. She disregarded studio orders and traveled to New York for President John F. Kennedy's May 19 birthday celebration at Madison Square Garden where emcee Peter Lawford poked fun at her reputation, calling her the "late" Marilyn Monroe. When Martin came down with a cold, she refused to work with him for three days until he recovered. On the days she did report to work, she often had trouble concentrating.

"We'd get reports from the psychiatrist. We'd get reports from the producer," remembered Bernstein. "If she did show up, it was like the second coming. Everybody did fall down and genuflect."

"We shot about seven weeks on *Something's Got to Give*, Marilyn Monroe's last unfinished picture. That was a terribly sad occasion, because she arrived on the set looking absolutely lovely and then found she had frightful difficulty in concentrating."

— Director George Cukor

"Her preoccupation with her private emotional difficulties made it an agony for her to come to the studio at all," reflected Cukor. "Even when she did, she might get sick or fall asleep in her dressing room and fail to report to the set anyhow. I think she knew she wasn't doing a good job when she did play a scene; and she therefore became more and more terrified of facing the camera."

Monroe had her good days. The day Cukor shot her nude scene was one with photographers on hand eager to snap the voluptuous celebrity. "Well, this is knocking Elizabeth Taylor off the cover of all the magazines," she happily bragged to producer Henry Weinstein.

She put in a full day on Friday, June 1, her 36th birthday, only to call in sick again the following Monday. The affable Martin had had enough. "It's the first time I saw Dean just get angry," Charisse recalled. "He started pacing the floor and George tried to calm him down.... After a while, he said, 'OK, that's it,' and he walked right off the set. That was it right there. That's when the picture stopped."

By June 6, when Monroe claimed illness once more, she had missed 13 of 30 days and the production was one million dollars over budget. Cukor wanted her replaced. On June 8, the studio filed a breach of contract suit against their wayward star and announced that *Something's Got to Give* would continue with Lee Remick taking over Monroe's part. An unhappy Martin quit, effectively killing the movie.

"He had not even wanted to do the picture, he told others; he had accepted only because 'Marilyn wanted me,'" the actor's biographer Nick Tosches would later write.

Opposite page: Having just declared Nick Arden's (Dean Martin) long missing wife, Ellen (Monroe), dead, the judge (John McGiver) marries Nick to his new bride, Bianca (Cyd Charisse). Top: Lita (Alexandra Heilweil) and Timmy (Robert Christopher Morley), don't realize the pretty stranger is their mother, Ellen, who disappeared when they were toddlers. Bottom: Caught between two lovers, Nick carries new bride Bianca over the threshold while his not-so-late wife watches.

Something's Got to Give might not have ended there. Even after the trauma she had just put the studio through, Fox wanted Monroe back and she was eager to get back to work. On August 1, Monroe signed a new million-dollar contract with the studio. Something's Got to Give would go back into production with Jean Negulesco replacing Cukor as director. Four days later, Monroe was dead. A year later, Move Over, Darling starring Doris Day and James Garner arrived in theaters, a remake of My Favorite Wife with a new script by Hal Kanter and Jack Sher. Even without a nude scene, it grossed nearly $13 million in theaters, becoming the hit Twentieth Century Fox wanted all along.

"She was not responding to the scenes. Swimming in a pool, playing with kids, that's all fun, but that's not going to make a movie."

— Something's Got to Give associate producer/art director Gene Allen

"I wanted our picture to be a great one, believe me. I really wanted it to be great. Then I got sick, and well, you know the rest of the story. The newspapers and magazines have been full of what happened, and now I'm waiting. Everything they've been saying in the press about me is not true. I hope I can continue *Something's Got to Give*. It can be successful — I know it can and so does everyone else connected with it."

— Monroe

Opposite page: The skinny dip that made international headlines. Top: "Did you enjoy your swim?" A dazzled Nick tries to play it cool with Ellen.

CONCLUSION

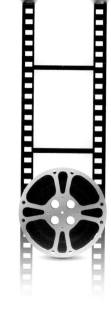

Even if you've never seen a Marilyn Monroe film, you know her greatest cinematic moments. The iconic images of Monroe in the dazzling strapless pink dress from *Gentlemen Prefer Blondes* (1953) or the white halter dress from *The Seven Year Itch* (1955) are part of the pop culture landscape, instantly recognizable to millions of people worldwide, even decades after her death.

Such is the reach of Monroe's influence that virtually every avenue of artistic expression, high and low, has explored her mythic stature. Legendary artist Andy Warhol made a series of silk screens of a Monroe publicity still that has become iconic in its own right. Serious writers such as Norman Mailer and Gloria Steinem have tried to capture and analyze Monroe's allure and what it says about society. Other writers have focused on the more sensational elements of Monroe's life and have churned out salacious biographies that sometimes promote conspiracy theories about her death.

Two years after she died, Monroe's ex-husband, Arthur Miller, unveiled his play *After the Fall* (1964) with a Monroe-esque central character. It was a commercial success, but his motives were questioned by reviewers. More than ten years later another play by Robert Patrick, *Kennedy's Children* (1975), featured a character who wanted to be Marilyn Monroe. Many lesser productions also came to life, including a failed musical version of the star's life.

While she was alive, several filmmakers created Monroe-inspired characters in their films. Frank Tashlin's satirical comedy *Will Success Spoil Rock Hunter?* (1957) casts Jayne Mansfield as a bosomy blonde sex symbol with artistic aspirations. And John Cromwell's *The Goddess* (1958), written by Paddy Chayefsky, paints a thinly veiled and unflattering portrait of Monroe in the character of Rita Shawn (Kim Stanley, who had originated the role of Cherie in *Bus Stop* on stage). In the years since Monroe has died, there have been numerous feature films inspired by Monroe, such as *Insignificance* (1985) starring Theresa Russell, and made-for-television biopics, such as *Marilyn, the Untold Story* (1980) starring Catherine Hicks, and *Blonde* (2001), based on the novel by Joyce Carol Oates.

The depth of Monroe's impact on pop culture is varied and rich. Many a celebrity, such as Madonna and model Anna Nicole Smith, have borrowed a page from Monroe's

Opposite page: Monroe in *Gentlemen Prefer Blondes* (1953). Top: Monroe in *Don't Bother to Knock* (1952).

"If I am a star, the people made me a star. No studio, no person, but the people did."

— Monroe

Monroe in *The Seven Year Itch* (1955).

playbook. Songwriters Elton John and Bernie Taupin were inspired to compose a hit song about Monroe, 1973's chart-topping "Candle in the Wind." Even Disney animators admitted that they modeled *Peter Pan*'s Tinker Bell after Monroe.

To this day, the demand for Monroe memorabilia remains strong. On the high end, there are those who will pay $6,500 for a Monroe-autographed program from President Kennedy's birthday celebration at Madison Square Garden. On the low end, there are those who will hand over a few dollars for a keychain with Monroe's likeness on it. In a world where Monroe's movies are easily accessible and her image remains ever present, it seems highly likely that the intoxicating mix of innocence, beauty and sexual allure that Marilyn Monroe brought to the screen will continue to enrapture audiences for generations to come.

"It's nice to be included in people's fantasies, but you also like to be accepted for your own sake."

— Monroe

"Sometimes I think it would be easier to avoid old age, to die young, but then you'd never complete your life, would you? You'd never wholly know yourself."

— Monroe

Top: Monroe in *Niagara* (1953). Bottom: Monroe and Laurence Olivier in *The Prince and the Showgirl* (1957).

FILMOGRAPHY

Scudda Hoo! Scudda Hay! (1948)

Dangerous Years (1948)

Ladies of the Chorus (1949)

Love Happy (1949)

A Ticket to Tomahawk (1950)

The Asphalt Jungle (1950)

The Fireball (1950)

All About Eve (1950)

Right Cross (1950)

Hometown Story (1951)

As Young as You Feel (1951)

Love Nest (1951)

Let's Make It Legal (1951)

Clash by Night (1952)

We're Not Married (1952)

Don't Bother to Knock (1952)

Monkey Business (1952)

O. Henry's Full House (1952)

Niagara (1953)

Gentlemen Prefer Blondes (1952)

How to Marry a Millionaire (1952)

River of No Return (1954)

There's No Business Like Show Business (1954)

The Seven Year Itch (1955)

Bus Stop (1956)

The Prince and the Showgirl (1957)

Some Like It Hot (1959)

Let's Make Love (1960)

The Misfits (1961)

Something's Got to Give (1962)